OUR STORIES CONNECT

OUR STORIES CONNECT

Creating Youth Storytelling Programs to Raise Confident, Compassionate, and Capable Leaders

A Children at the Well Guidebook

Editor

Paula B. Weiss

Cohoes Falls Media

Our Stories Connect: Creating Youth Storytelling Programs to Raise Confident, Compassionate, and Capable Leaders

All rights reserved. Published 2018.
Copyright © 2018 by WithOurVoice, Inc.
Cohoes Falls Media, PO Box 271, Latham NY 12110

Typeset by: Medlar Publishing Solutions Pvt Ltd., India

Print ISBN: 978-0-9981724-0-8
Ebook ISBN: 978-0-9981724-1-5

Dedicated in fond memory of:

Michelle (Micki) Groper (1951–2017)

Micki, a beloved wife, mother, teacher, religious educator, song leader, storyteller, and C@W story coach, was a wonderful woman who made a significant impact in her community.

Meir O'Brien (1997–2017)

Meir, a beloved son, grandson, brother, classmate, friend, and C@W alum, was about to enter his junior year at the University of Chicago. He had attended the Maimonides School in Albany, New York, and the American Hebrew Academy in Greensboro, North Carolina. His passion and dedication for thinking of others was unwavering, even until his untimely death. He was a political activist who had hopes of being a rabbi, lawyer, and governor of New York.

May they be remembered through their stories. May their memories be blessings forever.

Additionally, WithOurVoice, Inc. dedicates this guidebook to the founders, directors, coaches, and all of the young tellers of Children at the Well. The fabric of our community is stronger because of your enthusiastic commitment to the power of story to transform and unite, celebrating the multitude of ways our diverse stories do, in fact, connect.

WithOurVoice, Inc.

In 1993 a small cadre of individuals from around the Capital Region of New York State came together, under the leadership of Gert Johnson, to form the Interfaith Story Circle of the Tri-City Area (IFSC). Motivated by the love of story and its power to unite, this circle gathered people from a variety of religious and cultural traditions on a monthly basis to tell and listen to one another's stories of faith, life, family, and heritage. Thirteen years later, with the help of a grant from the National Storytelling Network, Children at the Well (C@W) was created to provide a similar space especially for youth. These neophyte tellers, guided by professional coaches, learned to identify, craft, and tell compelling stories. Through the process of discovering their voice they found confidence in themselves and a compassion, understanding and acceptance of those who were, at first, different. The C@W program has developed and transformed with experience. It is indeed a program whose shape molds around the participants involved.

The corporate entity WithOurVoice, Inc. formally unites IFSC and C@W under one leadership structure. Driven by a mission to promote understanding, respect, and friendship among people of diverse cultures, ethical traditions, and religious beliefs through the sharing of story, WithOurVoice, Inc. opens new space for future programs to emerge; ones that invite fresh voices from our community to surface.

Like quilted circles of fabric, sewn and crafted with care, these programs form the story quilt of our community. It is our hope that this guide will prove valuable in the formation of your own story circles into one community quilt of inclusion and peace.

Contents

Part 2: C@W Coaching Exercises

Micki Groper, Mary Murphy, Nancy Marie Payne

About the Contributors

Barbara Aliprantis enjoys telling everyone she began her life's journey as a storyteller by eavesdropping in utero. Her repertoire includes family stories of her Greek immigrant childhood, world folktales, and, for the younger set, her favorite picture books adapted for telling. The recipient of an NSN ORACLE Service Award, Barbara has also been honored at New York City Hall for "her distinguished body of work…for her commitment to sharing multi-cultural folklore and immigrants' experiences for both hearing and non-hearing audiences around the country."

Noa Baum is an Israeli storyteller and educator. Her memoir, *A Land Twice Promised: An Israeli Woman's Quest for Peace* (Familius LLC 2016), tells of her friendship with a Palestinian woman and her use of storytelling for peace building. Noa performs and teaches internationally. She holds an MA in Theater-in-Education from NYU and has received a Parents' Choice Recommended Award, a Storytelling World Award, an Anne Izard Storytellers' Choice Award, and the 2017 LDSPPA Praiseworthy Award for Best Individual Author Publication. More information: www.noabaum.com

Kevin D. Cordi, Ph.D. has told and taught in over 40 states and around the world. He founded the Voices of Illusion storytelling guild and Voices Across the World, bringing together more than 183 youth storytelling clubs in America, Canada, and Japan. The author of *Playing with Stories* and co-author of *Raising Voices*, he teaches narrative, education, and literacy classes at Ohio Northern University. More information: www.kevincordi.com

Norah Dooley is a storyteller, educator, critically acclaimed children's author, and the creator and project director of StoriesLive.org, a high school storytelling curriculum and story slam program. A co-founder of massmouth.org and the Greater Boston Story Slam series, she teaches storytelling to graduate students at Lesley University and an undergraduate storytelling class at Tufts. Norah has an M.Ed in Creative Arts in Learning from Lesley University and a BFA in Painting from Tufts University/Museum School.

Marni Gillard, author of *Storyteller, Storyteacher*, explores oral tales and poems with middle schoolers, developing character, community, and orality. Her CD, *Without a Splash: Diving into Childhood Memories*, contains moments of triumph and trauma in a girl's life. Marni's performances and workshops help people of all ages retrieve and share memories and ancient tales. More information: www.marnigillard.com

Michelle (Micki) Groper (1951–2017) used storytelling in her Sunday school class-room and, after performing at the Riverway Storytelling Festival, became a storyteller in earnest. She held a degree in Music from the University of Houston and a degree in Education from the Manhattan School of Music. She worked with children as a teacher, song leader, worship leader, Girl Scout leader, youth group advisor, and storytelling coach for C@W. With her husband of 45 years, Micki relocated to Florida in 2017.

Adah Hetko is a former youth participant in Children at the Well. After graduating from Oberlin College, she used storytelling extensively as the Tanenbaum Inter-religious Fellow with the Religious and Spiritual Life Office for two years at Vassar College. Adah is an MA student in the Borns Jewish Studies Program at Indiana University, where she studies Yiddish language and music, and continues to use her storytelling skills for presentations and performances.

Gert Johnson is a retired high school religious studies teacher in the Catholic tradition. She holds a BA (Sociology) from Nazareth College of Rochester and an MA (Theology) from St. Bernard's School of Theology and Ministry. She is the founder of the Interfaith Story Circle (Albany/Schenectady/Troy, New York), which is a program of WithOurVoice Inc.; the co-founder and past co-director of Children at the Well Youth Storytellers for Peace & Understanding; and Chair of the National Storytelling Network's Interfaith Discussion Group.

Mary Murphy is a writer and teller of stories, and a storytelling teacher. From its inception in 2006 until 2014, Mary was a storytelling coach at Children at the Well. She leads memoir projects, several of which have resulted in the participants writing books. Experience Mary's stories at murphywong.net, as well as at the StoryByStory channel on YouTube.

Nancy Marie Payne has been an environmental educator since 1980 and is certified in elementary education in New York State. A professional storyteller, she performs in schools and other venues in the Northeast. She conducts storytelling workshops for students, writers, and other storytellers. The author of the novel, *How I Came to Dowagiac*, she has worked with Children at the Well since 2007.

Ben Russell joined Children at the Well at age 14, in 2006, and fell in love with storytelling and different traditions. At the State University of New York at Albany, Ben double-majored in Religious Studies and Philosophy, while assisting in the Children at the Well program. Ben is now happy to share his interests and experience with new Children at the Well students as a head story coach.

Laura Simms is an award-winning performer, writer, and educator advocating storytelling as compassionate action for personal and community transformation. Laura is the Artistic Director of the Hans Christian Andersen Storytelling Center in NYC, founder of The

Center for Engaged Storytelling (new), contributing editor for *Parabola* magazine, member of the Council for Global Education (a UN NGO), and spoken word consultant for foundations and NGOs working in post disaster and conflicts. Her most recent book is *Our Secret Territory: The Essence of Storytelling*.

Paula B. Weiss is co-founder and director of Children at the Well. Paula has studied, researched, published, and taught in the field of literacy acquisition. Following a passion to help others construct meaning from text and find their voice, she's been an academic editor and currently edits the *Co-op Voice* newsletter. She holds a BA from the University of Virginia in Comparative Religion and an MS and CAS in Reading from SUNY at Albany.

Acknowledgments

The roots of all goodness lie in the soil of appreciation for goodness.
—Dalai Lama

With gratitude and appreciation, we are honored to acknowledge the many who have contributed to the success of Children at the Well (C@W) and have enabled us to begin propagating the program widely.

Of those who helped to initiate, run, and sustain C@W, our most profound thanks go to Gert Johnson, co-founder, past director, and friend par excellence; and the dedicated souls who have served as coaches: Marni Gillard, the late Micki Groper, Mary Murphy, Claire Nolan, Nancy Marie Payne, Ben Russell; and assistant coaches: Danielle Charlestin, Irene Ferrell, Allison Lerman-Gluck, Khalafalla Osman, and Aviva Rossman. We thank Kate Dudding and Joe Doolittle for so, so much. We thank all of the wonderfully brave student participants and their families for showing up and engaging, again and again, over the years. We thank the many clergypersons and other community members who have visited C@W as guest speakers. We thank the Interfaith Story Circle and the WithOurVoice Inc. board members past and present for their continuing support, and all our other regulars who provide an appreciative audience at C@W performances and are vivacious attendees at potlucks, picnics, and other gatherings. We thank those who have offered us venues in which to rehearse and perform, and we thank storytellers from all over the country who have taken C@W into their hearts.

We are grateful to Ann Ellery for assistance in development. We thank our funders—which have included The Arts Center of the Capital Region, the Suozzo Family Foundation, the Chobani Foundation, the Seymour Fox Memorial Foundation, Stewarts Shops, and the Carl Fund—as well as all those who have made donations as individuals and have come to our performances and thrown some bills into the collection basket. It all helps!

We thank all who contributed chapters to this volume; and we thank the "Starter Kit Committee" of Marni Gillard, Shubha Raj, and Annu Subramanian. Coaches Mary, Micki, and Nancy, along with Bonnie Beard, Sharifa Din, and Pete Shawhan, were part of earlier efforts to create this guidebook. In the manuscript preparation and publishing process, Jeannine Laverty, Amy Collins of New Shelves Books, and Vanessa Mickan have provided incredible and invaluable assistance.

Eternal love and gratitude to my family: Joe, Adah, and Eli Hetko, Eliana Theodorou, and my late, great friend Aviva Sela Kol.

Below are names of some of the donors who made possible the publication of this volume through a 2016 Kickstarter campaign. More are listed on childrenatthewell.org. All were essential in enabling us to bring our vision to fruition:

Sara Armstrong
Bonnie Beard
William and Linda Betz
Chris Colarusso and Rita Nolan
Karin Dagneau and Kevin McNeal
Mary Kate Codd and Robert Davidson
Carla DeRasmo and Ken Nercessian
Norah Dooley
Alden Joe Doolittle
Kathryn Dudding
Kenneth Eike
Marni Gillard
Rune Gjelberg
Douglas Glucroft and Anda Stelian
Nicolette Nordin Heavey

Adah Hetko
Muriel W. Horowitz
Gertrude Johnson
Carol Kerman
Yao Lei
Claire Nolan
Norman Perrin
Lani Peterson
Andrea Star Reese
Linda Russell
Sandor Schuman
Fran Stallings
Tricia Tauss
William Welton
Mary and Leo Wong

How to Use This Book

PAULA B. WEISS

A little over a decade since Children at the Well (C@W) began, participants from our earliest years have blossomed into confident young adults, many of whom are furthering our work of fostering peace and understanding. Our coaching staff is dedicated and seasoned; the program has made friends nationally and internationally; and we have welcomed new, young story coaches and many wonderful families into the C@W "clan."

We want to share our good fortune and our recipe for peace, understanding, and youth leadership. This book has been assembled to assist you in starting your own storytelling program based closely or loosely on our model, according to your local needs and resources. If you're not ready for a full-blown program, we encourage you to start with the pieces that seem right for you.

Part 1 provides the essentials you need to know about our program, including the guidelines that we ask all storytelling groups that use the C@W name to follow. The rest of the chapters in Part 1 are designed so that you can dip in and out, depending on your interests and needs. They offer insights into our approach to the coaching of storytellers, holding performances, constructing narratives, helping storytellers find their unique voice, and the experiences of coaches and storytellers involved in C@W and other programs.

Part 2 offers a wealth of practical exercises you can use to help storytellers choose stories or develop their own stories, and build their performance skills. You can use the sample forms, story prompts, activities, and checklists in the appendix in running your own program; they are all available for downloading at childrenatthewell.org. Also listed in the appendix are storytelling organizations and festivals that C@W has been involved with, to encourage you to reach out to these or find similar allies and opportunities for participation in your own area. Be sure to check out the recommended resources list if you want to dive deeper into the theory and practice of storytelling and running a storytelling group.

Most of the chapters were written by C@W personnel: co-founders and directors (Gert Johnson and me), story coaches (Marni Gillard, Micki Groper, Mary Murphy, Nancy Marie Payne, and Ben Russell), and former participants (Adah Hetko and, again,

Ben Russell). Five chapters were contributed by storytellers tangentially connected with C@W (Barbara Aliprantis, Noa Baum, Kevin Cordi, Norah Dooley, and Laura Simms), who each have particular wisdom to share regarding youth storytelling and the power of storytelling to build bridges and grow leaders.

As you peruse these materials, assess your community's situation. Where are the divides that need addressing? Are the gaps primarily religious, or are they economic, gender based, racial, political, cultural, or something else? What are your local resources: libraries and librarians, schools and teachers, congregations, clergy, peace and justice centers, cultural centers, folklore groups, associations of storytellers, arts councils? Is there a particular kind of story you think may be helpful for your participants to focus on sharing: family stories, folktales, fairy tales, cultural tales, religious stories, personal tales, or some or all of the above? (Ben Russell and I thank our workshop participants at the National Storytelling Conference in 2015 for these suggestions.)

What is your vision? Who and where are the participants you'd like to work with? How would you design your own youth (or adult) storytelling program to build bridges and make a difference in *your* community?

PART 1

The Principles and Practices
of C@W Storytelling

CHAPTER 1

Welcome!

PAULA B. WEISS

Our History

Children at the Well (C@W) was launched in 2006 by the Interfaith Story Circle, a program organized by a teacher named Gert Johnson around the compelling idea that sharing stories is a powerful way to connect people of different religions. The organization that oversees the Interfaith Story Circle and C@W has, over the years, broadened its mission to include connecting people of different cultures and philosophies. The Interfaith Story Circle, our "sister" program, has become involved in exciting local efforts to use story to address economic and LGBTQ issues, and racial healing.

Similarly, C@W's focus has broadened. We have embraced the added diversity of participants who don't adhere to a particular religious tradition or may not believe in a divine entity. The addition of more diverse voices has been an important part of the program's growth. In this chapter, as well as providing a grounding in the principles and practices of C@W, I will also share results from one of our recent forays into changing up our recipe for peace, understanding, and youth leadership (see "Surprises," below).

The name "Children at the Well" was inspired by Cherie Karo Schwartz's retelling of the biblical story of Isaac digging out his father Abraham's wells, which had been covered over. In the story, Isaac then significantly goes on to establish a new well that is indisputably his own, calling it Rehovot, "expansiveness." Israeli artist Yoram Raanan, who created a painting based on this part of the story, said, "The Talmud teaches that water is an allusion to the Torah itself. The digging of wells is a search to reveal and spread its wellsprings."[1]

In the same way that every village traditionally had its own sources of water, every culture has its own teachings. And in every culture, young people are drawn to learn about where they come from, and they want to make their own mark upon the world. To build on Raanan's explanation, wells can be seen as a metaphor for the depths of our traditions, for the depths inside each of us, and for the search to find a more authentic and pure inner expression.

The Essentials

What are the essentials of the C@W method? Here is a list of basics. We feel so strongly about their fundamental importance that if you choose to use "Children at the Well" or "C@W" in the name of your storytelling program, we ask that you adhere to these guidelines:

- Participants are young and diverse. They learn the art of storytelling from a faculty gifted in working with young people.
- The story coaches must also be diverse, and skilled in teaching storytelling or other theatre or spoken-word performance arts.
- Coaches and participants learn about and celebrate the diversity that each person brings to the group.
- The program aspires to be intergenerational; we seek involvement of family members through discussion groups, social gatherings, and volunteer opportunities. We invite family members to hear guest speakers, and we encourage participants to bring friends and family to performances. Such involvement supports, enriches, and magnifies the program while it builds community.
- Story coaches emphasize the use of appreciations—statements that reflect the storytellers' skills and the listeners' enjoyment—as a way to help students become their own teachers, noticing and learning from one another's artistic choices.
- C@W storytellers don't memorize stories word for word or read from a text (though there have been some special exceptions). As they perform, they take listeners on a journey of images and emotions. Energy and responses from a live audience deepen their telling.
- Participants choose their own stories—from their lives, traditions, or heritage. The stories might be folktales, family stories, personal tales, or stories from scripture. Although elsewhere storytellers often tell stories from cultures other than their own, in C@W it's important to "dig stories from our own well" to deepen connections to our countries and cultures of origin, for personal growth and development of authentic "voice" (see below). Choosing stories exclusively from one's own experience and culture also serves to avoid cultural appropriation.
- We're careful not to use stories that could cause harm by promoting stereotypes, perpetuating damaging myths, or denigrating a group of people, though we don't necessarily shy away from stories that involve controversy. Some stories that participants tell are powerful statements of suffering and injustice; the stories speak for themselves.
- Stories told at C@W events are intended to empower, to humanize, and to repair. As novelist Chimamanda Ngozi Adichie said:

> *Stories matter. Many stories matter. Stories have been used to dispossess and to malign, but stories can also be used to empower and to humanize. Stories can break the dignity of a people, but stories can also repair that broken dignity.*[2]

The Importance of Voice

The metaphorical use of the word "voice" underpins the work of C@W. It's a term from literary criticism and U.S. writing instruction, entirely applicable to storytelling, that indicates the ways in which an author (or storyteller) can be "heard" through his or her expression. Voice signals authenticity to readers and audiences. Voice isn't static; it evolves. In retelling the stories of others (with permission, if necessary), storytellers assume and adapt the voices of other storytellers. In refining their telling of a story over time, they develop and strengthen their personal stamp on it. In creating stories from their own lives, they further develop their voice.

A post by the University of Richmond's writing center puts it this way:

> *Voice is empowerment. In and out of the writing world, it gives students confidence and competence in writing and problem-solving tasks.*[3]

The post goes on to describe another feature of voice that is especially relevant to C@W storytelling: "It allows writers [and, we would add, storytellers] the ability to define and locate themselves relative to other discourses." For C@W storytellers, these other discourses can come from their various traditions (usually the past), from established storytellers (usually an older generation), and from other C@W participants (their contemporaries). Coming to recognize and develop one's individual voice by honing the "ability to define and locate [oneself] relative to other discourses," in community with other voices, is an essential key to the community-building leadership the C@W program engenders.

Goals

Here are two anecdotes that offer glimpses into the goals of C@W. The first is from our volunteer webmaster, storyteller Kate Dudding, who in 2005 suggested we create a proposal for a youth program and submit it for the NSN Brimstone Award, which we subsequently won, enabling us to launch in 2006. Her anecdote encapsulates the togetherness that the C@W program inspires. (For those who aren't aware of the Village of Chelm and the Eastern European Jewish folklore tradition of wise-fool stories set there, know that it's a place of delight for all lovers of nonsense.)

> *What is most heartwarming to me and touches my soul is watching these young storytellers of Children at the Well before and after the program. They group together, chattering away, gesturing dramatically, and laughing often. All these young people from so many different cultures are now friends.*

> *One day, I was at a local story swap with three of the young men: a Hindu, a Jew, and a Muslim. Of course, they were sitting together. After several stories*

had been shared, there was a lull. The facilitator looked at them and said, "Does one of you have a story you'd like to share?"

Ritam turned to Ben and said excitedly, "Tell them a Chelm story!"

Khalafalla smiled and agreed, "Yes, tell them a Chelm story!"

So Ben did, and we all laughed at the tale.

I remember thinking: How many places in the world today would you find a Jew, a Hindu, and a Muslim sitting down together as friends and sharing stories?

Then I thought: Who would ever have imagined that one path to world peace goes directly through the village of Chelm?

The second glimpse into C@W is my observation of one youth storyteller's development of voice and confidence, and the empathy and understanding she elicits from her audience with her story. Demure, petite, and ever-agreeable, Shadeh, 18, had been choosing to tell traditional tales that professed her strong belief in Islam, or were funny and lighthearted. But in her final year in Children at the Well, Shadeh decided to take a risk and create a story of the recent history of her father's beleaguered land, the Province of Nuristan, in Afghanistan. It was a story about war, terror, and sudden death, but it was also about strong family ties and friendships. It wasn't an easy project for one so sunny; she had to work hard to find the right balance of light and shade to craft and tell the story effectively.

As she told at the final performance, dressed in a striking blue traditional costume, the audience was spellbound. Shadeh's mother later reported that her husband had had tears in his eyes as he listened. Another audience member reported that learning Shadeh's family history was "surprising and amazing." Shadeh herself seemed to have grown in gravity and stature with the telling of the story.

A few years into the program, we adopted the full name Children at the Well Youth Storytellers for Peace & Understanding. Although the ultimate goal of the program is peace and understanding among all peoples of the world (a lofty goal, for sure!), we begin with the communities at hand. We intentionally work to connect religious communities, schools, and individual families. We connect participants to one another, and we mentor participants as individuals and develop their capacity for peace building.

It's often said that true understanding begins with examining one's inner self and that peace begins in one's own heart. Young people are usually at the very beginning of those journeys; nevertheless, their energy and capacity for idealism make them ideal peace ambassadors. As C@W participants create connections with other participants and staff, and learn about the journeys of others, they gain insight into who they are and where they fit in. Meanwhile, they create bridges between the communities they are a part of and those of their fellow participants.

C@W participants are encouraged to look for a story that grabs them. Rarely do they understand right away what it is about the story that speaks to them. For tellers of all ages, that insight might gradually emerge in the process of working with the tale, or even after telling it numerous times. Once the telling comes together successfully, it can be enormously satisfying and lead to personal peace.

Similarly, when young people reach an understanding of their values and opinions, and realize the ways those might differ from someone else's, they've reached a solid foundation on which to build confidence in themselves and empathy for others. Understanding oneself and others, newfound appreciation for one's heritage and that of others, empathy, confidence, and articulate leadership—these are the goals our program seeks to help participants achieve.

Surprises

Our first surprise was that many students returned year after year. Some became especially proficient storytellers and spokespeople, traveling to tell stories, represent the program, and give workshops in storytelling and interfaith understanding. This helped us promote the program to possible donors and recruit new students, staff, and volunteers.

Some former participants have surprised us with inspired ideas to form other storytelling programs, using C@W as a model. The late Meir O'Brien, a 2009 C@W participant, was a young man with many progressive dreams. After leaving C@W, he attended the American Hebrew Academy (AHA) in Greensboro, North Carolina, a boarding high school that describes itself as "conservative, reform, conservadox, orthodox, and every Jew in between. We're Jewish and that's that." In his second year at AHA, Meir envisioned a C@W program there helping students from different walks of Jewish life learn about each other's journeys. Although this dream of Meir's has not yet materialized, in our opinion it's the type of brilliant adaptation that would have a great chance of succeeding if attempted.

Parents and friends of parents have been a surprising source of ideas and moral support. Some have recruited participants, joined the board, organized potlucks, and helped identify grant opportunities. Some have come to Interfaith Story Circle meetings and found they really enjoyed sharing stories.

Story coaches have been drawn to the program and have stayed dedicated for years. There has been good continuity and communication as the coaching personnel has gradually evolved.

We have also been surprised by some challenges as we've grown. I offer the following description of our recent efforts to evolve as encouragement for other groups to do the same as they become established, and as a reminder to "expect the unexpected."

As the program approached the ten-year mark, some changes were proposed to further increase diversity of participants and diversity in approaches to storytelling. That year, the coaching sessions were moved into town, to the First Unitarian Universalist

Society of Albany, to see if new connections could be made. Two fantastic assistant coaches with expertise in theatre and spoken word were hired. The following year, we began a "traveling troupe" of students who went out into the community regularly to tell stories. This year, in addition to a small traveling troupe, another C@W group met on Wednesdays at a public library as part of a pilot program created with the Refugee and Immigrant Support Services of Emmaus (RISSE) organization of Albany. C@W participants in the Wednesday group were mostly from RISSE's after-school program; they were joined by other local students.

As the age limit for the RISSE after-school program was 13, our C@W group ended up being younger than usual for us. Their ages ranged from nine to 13, and they happened to all be girls, which was also different from what we were used to. On the whole, the pilot was a success, but when C@W was invited to continue working with RISSE, it was agreed by all that modifications needed to be made to the program. Some of the challenges were logistical, having to do with factors such as the age range of the participants, scheduling, and the awkwardness of bringing the group from the RISSE site to the library each week. But other challenges went deeper. It became clear that even more preparation of staff would be necessary, especially more advance contact with RISSE participants at the site of their after-school program, well before the C@W season began. We decided that we would offer some storytelling performances there for all of their students to enjoy. This would ensure that coaches would be more fully informed about the RISSE experience and the individual students, and that the RISSE students would have a better idea about what was in store if they were to join the C@W program.

We realized that in coaching, we needed to use more group activities than usual. We also came to realize that we had been naïve about the extent to which some of these younger students from recently arrived families may be ready to share their culture publicly.

Assessing this pilot also drove home the many synergistic benefits of the contact we had with families in the past. We came to see how important to C@W's success such support has been, and we realized that we cannot take it for granted. In this pilot, we hadn't had a chance to meet any of the RISSE students' parents. It was clear that the RISSE students were not practicing their stories at home, and most family members were not able to attend the final story circle when the girls told their stories. We were fairly certain that parents were unaware of the aims of our program and did not know how to support it at home. The C@W staff lacked the richer understanding of students that comes with getting to know their families. We have since talked about ways to improve contact with families when we face similar circumstances in the future.

Structure

From C@W's beginning, we chose to separate administrative tasks from coaching responsibilities, employing one or two directors as well as coaches. That decision has added a layer of organizational complexity that presents challenges as well as benefits. As much as it provides a stronger team for vision setting, creative problem solving, and community outreach, it limits our flexibility and means we need to find compensation for more staff.

We found early on that to sustain the program in this configuration we would need to find a fiscal sponsor, partner with an established group, or form a nonprofit and gain tax-exempt status so that we could directly seek out grants and other funding. We took the latter route, which has allowed us to sustain our work at the present level, and we're still learning how to develop a healthy board and provide the support our program needs.

Other ways of structuring a youth storytelling program will no doubt be more suited to different circumstances. Here are a few alternatives, in ascending order of complexity:

1. Workshops using C@W techniques can be held within a preexisting structure. These workshops can be provided by staff or outside consultants, supported by organizational programming funds. An example of this approach can be found in chapter 12, about Adah Hetko's work at Vassar College.

2. A basic ongoing youth storytelling group could possibly be operated with no budget whatsoever, as Cordi and Sima point out in their book, *Raising Voices*.[4] This would generally mean that story coaches volunteer their time or are compensated from another source, such as a school, and cooperating organizations—such as schools, libraries, congregations, and community centers—provide space, advertising, and other logistical support. Opportunities for travel and enrichment may be limited, though the freedom from the need for ongoing fundraising and board involvement makes this an option worth considering. Sima and Cordi also suggest training advanced students to become assistant coaches.

3. In another scenario, a minimal budget to provide compensation for coaches, supplies, and/or enrichment could be funded directly by storytelling activities undertaken by coaches and students. In chapter 9 of *Raising Voices*, Sima and Cordi give a number of appealing examples of how this can be accomplished. See Kevin Cordi's contribution in this book, chapter 10, for a discussion of engaging participants in program management.

4. Partnering with an existing organization such as a community youth arts center or an interfaith center or council that seeks programming that aligns with its mission could provide greater structure and resources while minimizing administrative duties. This would most likely involve board oversight and group decision-making, adding to the complexity of the arrangement.

Allies

We encourage you to look around your communities and beyond to seek out resources and partnering possibilities. A grant from the National Storytelling Network (NSN) gave our program its start, and informal partnerships with area organizations made it possible to build on that start. The Capital Region of New York, where we are located, has a strong storytelling community, a strong history of interfaith relations and organizations, and a thriving arts community.

We form connections and friendships with clergy, teachers, storytellers, and people in the local media. Community and state organizations—including chambers of commerce, community foundations, and statewide organizations such as the New York Council on Nonprofits—offer assistance to fledgling nonprofits. We continue to seek opportunities to learn about and connect with aligned programs, especially other youth programs.

Further afield, we connect with the Interfaith Youth Core, which is based in Chicago; the Hickey Interfaith Center of Nazareth College in Rochester, New York; Youth Leaders Engaging Across Differences (Youth LEAD) of Sharon, Massachusetts, and their TIDE Confer-ence; the Brave New Voices Network of Youth Speak, based in California's Bay Area; and the National Storytelling Network and its regional affiliate, Northeast Storytelling (NEST - formerly LANES). We also participate in an array of storytelling festivals and music festivals that include storytelling. A list of such festivals, storytelling and interfaith organizations, and other organizations helpful to us appears at the end of the book.

In Sum

It's been an ongoing adventure with equal parts fun, joy, and hard work. We are amply rewarded by seeing people young and older build friendships, gain confidence, and come into their own. Being part of the wonderful connections forged through C@W makes our efforts worthwhile.

We really do hope you'll feel encouraged and empowered by this book to launch a program of your own. Assess your community's needs and resources, and try the parts that appeal to you. We are looking forward to having you as partners in this work!

Endnotes

1. Raanan, Yoram, "Isaac Re-digs His Father's Wells," November 9, 2015, http://www.yoramraanan.com/single-post/2015/11/09/Isaac-ReDigs-His-Father's-Wells.
2. Adichie, Chimamanda Ngozi, "The Danger of a Single Story," TED talk, July 2009, https://www.ted.com/talks/chimamanda_adichie_the_danger_of_a_single_story.
3. University of Richmond writing center, http://writing2.richmond.edu/training/project/voice/voicedef.html.
4. Sima, J. and K. Cordi. 2003. *Raising Voices: Creating Youth Storytelling Groups and Troupes.* Westport, Conn.: Libraries Unlimited.

CHAPTER 2

The Power of Story

It is such a joy to see our youth take their place in our community and in the world as ambassadors of peace and understanding. Through them we touch the future.

—Gert Johnson

In response to questions posed by Paula Weiss, C@W co-founder and director, Gert Johnson writes about the ideas underpinning C@W, reflects on the outcomes for young people and parents whose lives have been touched by the program, and offers helpful observations for those setting up youth storytelling groups in their own communities.

Paula Weiss: *Thirteen years before we co-founded C@W, you began the Interfaith Story Circle (IFSC) in 1993. In your quest to bring people of diverse backgrounds together to get acquainted and learn from one another, why did you choose to use stories? Do you continue to believe in the power of story?*

Gert Johnson: In the early 1990s, I did graduate work in narrative theology, validated the use of story for moral and religious education in my master's thesis, and began to use it in my high school classroom. This experience transformed my teaching. It taught me that story was a compelling and powerful bridge between teacher and student and among young people who were very different from one another. It left me curious to know if story could break down barriers and build community among adults of different religious and moral traditions. The answer was yes, it could. Over the past 25 years, those of us in the IFSC and C@W have experienced the inspirational moral and healing power of story among people of diverse religions (Hindus, Jews, Christians, Muslims), ethical traditions, and cultures. Even today, with all the turmoil in our world, we continue to have confidence and take comfort in the power of story-sharing to bring about friendship, peace, and understanding.

PW: *What were the factors (people, organizations, and other resources) that enabled you to successfully co-found, direct, and grow C@W?*

GJ: Paula Weiss and I were partners in launching and administering this program. Having each other to brainstorm ideas, make decisions, and deal with issues that arose was a great strength. We drew upon each other's gifts and greatly valued our mutual support.

We intentionally chose as coaches storytellers who take a noncritical, appreciative, student-centered approach. I believe this has been vital to our success. With any group of teens it's important to create a safe space and to establish an atmosphere of appreciation and mutual respect. This is even more true with teens who are diverse. They may be a bit uncomfortable at first with people whose traditions and cultures are foreign to theirs. The fact that our coaches were already experienced in coaching youth was a big advantage.

The guidelines for the proposal we wrote for the National Storytelling Network (NSN) required that we solicit letters of support from communities that would commit to our program the first year. We received letters from a Catholic high school, a Hindu temple, The Jewish Federation, and a Muslim school. NSN's requirement turned out to be a blessing. We had our ducks in a row before beginning to operate.

We started by having teachers from those four communities nominate students. Teachers know their students. They understand that it is not necessarily the students who are academic achievers who will be good storytellers. They can identify those who may have a gift for storytelling or who need, or will love, it the most.

Parental involvement and support helped us to grow and have been a major factor in the students staying with us from year to year. From the start, we invited parents not only to listen to guest tellers who shared with the students but also to gather with one another while their children were being coached. Sometimes they read and discussed wisdom tales from *Doorways to the Soul* by storyteller Elisa Davy Pearmain. At other times, we met with them at a nearby coffee house where they shared stories of their religious or cultural journeys. Their sharing created strong bonds. It also prompted a deeper involvement in C@W. A good number of parents are still with us 11 years later: they direct C@W, serve on the board, create flyers for our events, and plan interfaith story circles.

PW: *Many other youth storytelling programs are led by storytellers who are working directly with participants. Would you please explain why you structured the program to have directors leading the staff of story coaches and discuss how you feel this arrangement has worked over the years?*

GJ: That design allowed Paula and I to work on program operations, development, publicity, fundraising, communications, and parental involvement. Mary Murphy and Marni Gillard focused on coaching. Because we faced so many decisions while establishing policies during the first year, we all met weekly or bi-weekly. We used conference calls to accommodate our busy schedules.

Looking back, I wish that we had not been so quick to draw the lines of responsibilities. We realized later that coaches can offer help with attendance, communicating with students as issues arise, and on upcoming events such as fundraisers. The coaches are the ones closest to the students. They meet students weekly, so they have the opportunity to communicate plans and needs, encourage commitment, and develop group spirit.

I will note, having administrators to work on parent involvement turned out to be a great strength. One of our parents often made a point of expressing her gratitude for that. She explained that such involvement was unique among the programs her children belonged to. It made all the difference to her and her family.

Our eventual work in the broader community—having students attend and present at a variety of programs and events—was also brought about at our administrative level.

PW: *You served as C@W's community liaison for a number of years. What are your thoughts about the importance of reaching out to new communities, and what do you see as some practical ways to go about this?*

GJ: Continually searching for and reaching out to new communities has been a hallmark of IFSC and C@W. We are always on the lookout for students in school, religious education, interfaith, cultural, or community programs.

It has been helpful to attend programs and events where there may be interested parties. For example, we made our first contact with the Hindu community by going to hear a Hindu teller who came to perform at the temple. One of our students joined as the result of our attendance at an interfaith dinner, another because of our participation in a Brahma Kumaris evening of meditation.

Some of our youth have become interested as a result of a C@W dress rehearsal for an upcoming performance being held at one of their classes, or of our students coming to perform at their religious services.

Stepping Toward the Lion: Finding My Story, the award-winning 30-minute film that was created by one of our C@W students, has been an excellent way to introduce people to the C@W program. DVDs are available for this purpose. For a copy, please contact us through childrenatthewell.org.

PW: *What do you see as C@W's main benefits to participants, families, staff, and community?*
GJ: I'm happy to answer that question! I see a number of main benefits:

• First, being coached in the art of storytelling allows students to discover their gifts and talents at a young age. It gives them pride of self and a developing ease with public speaking that spills over into their school life and work and into their preparation for college. (One of our students used a video of a C@W presentation she was in as part of her successful college application.) In the future, no matter what career or activities our students pursue, whenever they are called on to speak they will have the ability to be at ease and enliven their presentation with story.

- Second, adolescence is often a time when young people reject their family's beliefs and culture—whatever they have been raised with that makes them feel "different." Most participants in C@W delve into their traditions as they choose and work on their stories, and end up with a deeper appreciation of their heritage and pride in who they are.

- Third, C@W students learn not to be afraid of being with people who are different from them. They find on the contrary that learning about difference is good, something to be sought out. I have had many students tell me that this was true for them. C@W prepares them to take their place in our globally interdependent world.

- Fourth, the C@W staff takes great pleasure in watching the young people grow, develop their storytelling skills, and learn to be representatives of their cultures and religious traditions. Over the years, several storytellers have joined the staff of C@W on a volunteer basis because they admire the program, its mission, and the young people involved.

- Last, the youth draw the adults in, just as we had hoped. Parents, family, and friends look forward to seeing the young people shine at our community events. The students' joy in their friendship with each other is palpable. They model for us adults what it means to break down stereotypes and rejoice in diversity. I remember one parent who told a story of speaking up for Muslims when disparaging remarks about them were made in her presence. Not a Muslim herself, she knew from her C@W participation that what was being said was not true. She said she saw the world differently as a result of being a part of C@W.

PW: *What do you wish you and those you were working with had known when first starting the program?*

GJ: I'm ready for this one, too! The first of my answers is about fun, several are organizational matters, and one is about having faith in the students:

- Socializing at the start with something like a pizza party and fun exercises pays off. Don't dive right into the coaching.

- It's not a bad idea to start with a few too many students, as some may decide to drop out.

- On the other hand, trying to handle too many students in the program can be problematic. The coach-to-student ratio is important to consider. In past years, we found that two coaches and an assistant or two, and approximately 15 students was about right for us.

- We learned we had to set an attendance policy while also remaining flexible to student and family needs. Absences affect preparation for performance. In some cases, students were not ready to tell.

- We had to figure out the best way to communicate with parents. Even after obtaining all email addresses and phone numbers, we needed to know which communication method was the most likely to work.
- We learned to make a concentrated effort to help students understand their stories early in the program. Because they need to be able to converse about their story as well as tell it, we learned to have them think about and discuss their story's source, the wisdom they feel the story shares, and its connection to their personal life and their cultural or religious tradition.
- We have to avoid long stories so that audiences don't grow restless. Five-to-seven-minute stories are ideal. For some students, an even shorter story can provide the path to success. Because short stories can pack a punch, they can give confidence to a first-time teller.
- Finally, we need to deeply believe that worrying about the students' differing abilities is needless. Students need to know that the audience is going to appreciate each one of them if they have worked hard and are brave enough to tell.

PW: *Is there anything else you would like to add?*

GJ: It is a pleasure for all involved with IFSC and C@W to step into the world of story. Here is a reflection of a first-time attendee at one of our intergenerational community events that illustrates that pleasure:

> *It was my first time at a formal telling event. I had been to one previous story circle. There was no iPhone, no cell phones, and no computers. It was just a big diverse group of people from different faiths listening to each other's stories, smiling, laughing, and sharing peace and hope. Hope for today and a better tomorrow. It is easy to get lost in all the negativity in the world. Sometimes it is nice to take a step back and feel the good and gentle spirit of who we are as people, and see our young poised for tomorrow. How lucky for me I was there! My heart was opened by the wonderful spirit of these young people. They touched me—I will be back.*
>
> —Pamela A. Mertz

CHAPTER 3

Fundamentals of C@W
Story Coaching

MICKI GROPER, MARY MURPHY, NANCY MARIE PAYNE

In this chapter, we're going to look at the basics of coaching young storytellers using the C@W approach, including ideas for organizing groups and structuring coaching sessions.

How Are the C@W Students Found?

C@W participants range in age from 11 to 18. Initially, to gather an interfaith group with access to students, Gert Johnson conducted workshops about story, for teachers of religion. Those teachers nominated the first C@W students. Through the years the practice of having teachers or leaders from the community nominate students has continued to be successful.

Over time, we've noticed that the most successful C@W participants are not necessarily the very best students in school, or the best readers or writers. Sometimes they are, of course, but not always. We've found that it can be the kids who have the most to say, or those who seem to need this type of expressive outlet the most, who put their all into the program and get the most out of it. Keep this in mind when discussing recruitment with teachers and other adults, and let them know.

Nominated students are sent an invitation to write a letter about themselves and their reasons for wanting to join C@W (see appendix for a sample letter). When we receive a student's note it demonstrates to us that the desire to join comes directly from the young person. The process gives students an awareness of the commitment they'll be making. Their responses are shared among staff as a way to begin getting to know the new students. Letters are then sent in return, welcoming each letter writer into the program.

Recruitment of new students can be assisted by everyone involved in the program, including board members, staff, parents of current participants, and participants themselves. Continual outreach, both formal and informal, introduces new groups and people to the program. Maximum diversity is a goal, and this helps to accomplish that.

What Experience Do C@W Coaches Need?

An essential element of C@W is that our coaches are professionals who are known for their good work with young people. Some have been teachers, storytellers, spoken word artists, youth program directors, youth theatre directors, librarians, and religious school educators. They have strong storytelling skills and experience with performance. It's important that coaches come from a variety of cultures and faith traditions.

What Is the Time Commitment for a Coach?

Staff meets once before the season begins to review the past year and plan for the new. During the coaching season, they meet about once a month, and they have a wrap-up meeting soon after the final performances. Coaches sometimes meet on their own, and they touch base about 45 minutes before each group coaching session to make last-minute preparations.

The C@W season lasts about four months, January through April. During this time, students and coaches meet once a week for 2.5-hour coaching sessions on Sunday afternoons, which seem to present the fewest scheduling conflicts.

Occasionally students need coaching outside the regular sessions when they've been invited somewhere to perform or need extra help before a final performance. This coaching entails additional compensation for the coach. After letting the director know that some extra coaching is called for, the coach will arrange to meet with the student at a library or other convenient location. (Use the Events Form in the appendix to keep track of additional coaching sessions.) Throughout the year, the director will occasionally call on coaches to assist with organizing or attending a satellite performance or appearance, as well.

Where Is Coaching Held?

Weekly full-group C@W coaching sessions have been held in public libraries, schools, and churches. Cozy pizza parties were often held in the homes of staff members. At one point it was decided to relocate the coaching sessions with the goal of drawing more participants from an urban neighborhood.

The weekly coaching space needs to be:

- Centrally located, with easy enough access.
- Affordable.
- Large enough. There must be a space big enough for the entire group, including an area for some limited physical exercise, as well as room for small groups to work simultaneously without being a distraction to one another.
- Food friendly. It's important that the venue allow food so that snacks can be brought in.

Elements of the Coaching Process

Coaching begins with planning for a successful experience for the students. Much thought is put into how coaches will organize students into groups, interact with them, and model behavior for them. Here are the essentials of the C@W coaching program.

Grouping the Students

In the early years, students of various ages and experience levels were mixed to give students as much varied interaction as possible. Eventually, students were grouped homogeneously according to the length of their tenure in the program. Students who had been in the program for two or more years were given additional roles and activities, such as organizing the large performances or doing satellite appearances. Alumni who remain in the area may be invited to rejoin the group as coaching assistants.

Group cohesion is important, because the season's success depends on how well all bond at the beginning. During the first meeting, the students get to know each other through a pizza party and icebreaking and team-building exercises.

At each weekly coaching session, all the students first come together for large-group coaching, and then split up into separate groups for small-group coaching.

Variety in Coaching

Groups are rotated so students come to work with all of the coaches to experience the diversity of the coaching staff.

Story Choice

Students choose stories they want to learn to tell. They're encouraged to find stories that "speak" to them by:

- Asking for help from their parents, grandparents, religious leaders, or other elders in their communities.
- Interviewing others for this purpose (ethnographic interviews). This is a skill that has been taught in workshops.
- Looking into religious texts or books of folk or fairy tales.
- Thinking about situations or events in their own lives or in their family history.

It's suggested that first-year students begin learning storytelling by choosing an already composed tale and attempt a personal tale for their next story if they wish to.

Students are taught to choose or create stories that:

- contain wisdom and are connected to their heritage
- are appropriate to tell to a diverse audience (See Guidelines for Choosing Stories, in the appendix).

Coaches make sure they and the students are familiar with the origins of traditional tales students have chosen. Students are asked to complete a Story Choice Form (see appendix) about the story they have chosen. This helps them begin to articulate their personal connections to the stories.

Other key points about story choice are:

- **Story length.** Students are guided to aim for a maximum telling time of 5–7 minutes per story. This helps them find a shape for their story. A secondary reason for limiting length is audience enjoyment at performances.
- **Story strength.** Students are coached to avoid summing up "The Moral" of a story in a telling. Listeners bring their own personalities and experiences to bear in their interpretations of a story's message. When a moral is dictated to them it diminishes the power of a story.
- **Storytelling ethics.** If students have chosen stories created by others, they're made aware of the importance of securing specific permissions, when necessary, from storytellers and/or authors for live telling in performance, for making recordings, and for posting the recordings online.

In coaching sessions and in staff meetings, staff members discuss story length, story strength, and sensitive issues the stories may bring up.

Skills

Coaches help students learn to:

- modify their stories for successful telling
- use their voices and their bodies for storytelling
- develop authentic voice and express themselves with power
- give helpful feedback to others in the form of "appreciations"

Active listening skills are taught through games. Active listening includes facing the speaker, looking at the speaker, focusing on the speaker's words, and giving the speaker feedback. The coaches insist on silence during a story rehearsal.

Appreciations

Students must feel safe and comfortable within the group. They are taught to watch for particular strengths—skillful storytelling techniques—in one another's rehearsals.

Positivity is emphasized in all interactions. The first reaction to any telling is in the form of appreciations—statements that reflect the teller's skills and the listeners' enjoyment of the tale. The giving of specific appreciations must be frequently modeled and emphasized. Appreciations are a potent kind of positive response because they're the building blocks to success with any story.

Modeling

Coaches are role models. They show interest in learning about other traditions and take care to learn and use correct pronunciation of key terms and texts and participants' names. They share stories from their own traditions.

In the large-group setting, coaches might share how they're working on a story and talk about the decisions they're grappling with in developing that story. They take turns to show a variety of storytelling styles.

Centering

Coaching sessions begin with a centering reflection or meditation and often end with a prayer or other reading offered by a participant. The sources of these texts are noted.

Guest Speakers

It's important for the students to hear from, and have a chance to interact with, people who use storytelling in their work. Four or five guest speakers come in each season, throughout February and March.

Guests may come in early to observe coaching sessions, though they usually arrive during snack time and mingle. Guests are generally given 30 minutes to address the group, though some, due to the nature of their presentation and perhaps the distance they've traveled to be there, deserve a 50-minute slot. Guests are told the amount of time they'll have when they're invited. Coaching times are rearranged to make time for the guests (see suggested schedules at the end of this chapter).

Coaches introduce the guests and participate. Parents and others are invited to hear the guest speakers, and question-and-answer time as well as informal conversation are always part of the visits. Each guest is encouraged to tell a story or lead a story-related exercise.

Guest speakers have included clergy, therapists, psychologists, professors of business, spoken word artists, storytellers, writers, historians, and a physicist. Care is taken to include guests from as many of the communities represented by the students as possible. At times, guests from unrepresented traditions are invited; these further expand the group's knowledge and understanding.

Planning a C@W Coaching Season

To help you plan your own season of C@W coaching, here is an outline of how C@W structures its coaching sessions and staff meetings. For the exercises that are mentioned, you can find instructions in part 2 of this book.

First Meeting of the Year

- Review the calendar for the new season and set up a timeline.
- Conduct an orientation for new coaches and assistants.
- Review what else is new for the season.
- Review the list of incoming students and establish student groups.
- Generate suggestions for guest speakers and locations for rehearsals, performances, satellite performances, and appearances.
- Plan the first coaching session.

Coaches' Weekly Pre-coaching Session Meetings

- The following tasks are assigned: Who will lead the opening reflection? Give announcements? Lead discussions and lead story exercises?
- The order of the coaching session is planned.
- It is decided who will coach each group.
- Coaches brief one another on students' individual and collective successes and progress.
- The following week's session and upcoming performances are discussed.

The Coaching Session

1. **Reflection** (approximately 3 minutes)
   Seated in a circle, participants are asked to center themselves and focus on the tasks of becoming better storytellers and on helping one another become better storytellers. With closed eyes, the group practices conscious breathing and listens as an inspirational text is read. The origins of the texts used are identified for educational purposes.
2. **Announcements and Journals** (approximately 10 minutes)
   - **Announcements**
     - Coaches may announce reminders of important upcoming dates, appreciation of student and coach accomplishments, lists of performers for a specific program, etc.
     - If there's something special going on in a student's congregation or other community, it's mentioned during this time.

- **Journals**
    - Each participant is given a journal. They are asked to record their progress, what they want to improve, what they want to add or change, etc. They record reactions of their peers to their stories, along with coaching suggestions.
    - The journals are given out at meetings and collected at the end of the day, unless a student asks to take his or her journal home. All students take their journals home at the end of the season.
    - Keeping a journal is an excellent way to keep track of one's repertoire and record ideas, techniques, appreciations, and suggestions. It's hoped that students will continue to use this tool.

3. **Vocal and Physical Warm-ups** (approximately 10 minutes)

To perform successfully, a storyteller must feel comfortable in a physical sense. The storyteller's instrument is the entire body, especially the parts that produce the voice, and the instrument must be kept in good condition. Vocal and physical exercises each week free the voice and body from the tensions of everyday use and allow the storyteller to express a full range of emotion, mood, and meaning, and extend vocal range and breath control. As Kristin Linklater wrote:

> Physical awareness and relaxation are the first steps in the work to be done, with a constant emphasis on mind-body unity. Breath and sound must always be connected to thought and feeling so that the two processes work simultaneously to activate and release inner impulses and to dissolve physical blocks.[1]

Each coaching session should include at least one physical and one vocal exercise.

4. **Large-Group Coaching** (approximately 20 minutes*)

Initially, exercises involve getting to know one another and feeling comfortable in the group. Prompts are used to encourage spontaneous storytelling (see appendix for a list of prompts).

Over the next couple of weeks, the focus moves to helping students choose an appropriate story.

Later in the season, exercises cover learning a story, creating characters, using imagination, movement and gestures, voice projection, voice characterization, and the use of microphones. Also included are exercises to develop performance techniques such as making eye contact, involving audiences in the telling, and launching a story and ending it cleanly and with strength.

5. **Snack** (10–15 minutes)

Snack breaks are weekly opportunities for group socializing. Coaches stay available and, as needed, encourage the seasoned students to approach new or shyer students to bring them into a group. Over the years the older students have begun doing this without being told. Staff keep an eye out to encourage mixing in general, as students who are used to being together will naturally seek one another out and resist mixing with the others.

Coaches may follow up on things students say during this downtime. They may ask a student to share his or her thoughts or insights with the group when it reassembles, incorporate a student's ideas into a session (always giving credit to the student) or give positive on-the-spot feedback. Interactions during this time help build a stronger bond within the group.

When providing snacks, ethnic, religious, and dietary needs must be taken into consideration.

6. **Small-Group Coaching** (approximately 60 minutes*)

Individual style is important; no two tellers or tellings are alike. In the same way, there is no perfect way to coach. Coaches must wipe out past judgments and listen to each teller with a "beginner's mind."

Politeness and respect for the person telling a story are emphasized, and coaches and students offer appreciations after a telling.

Well-placed questions by coaches are empowering:

- Questions such as "What do you want help with?" or "What would you like us to listen for?" make the listener a partner in the coaching.
- Questions such as "What do you love about this story?" and "What do you want to convey to the audience?" and "What are the character's motivations?" help them clarify the focus of the tale.

During the small-group session:

- Coaches offer suggestions on how to get to the next level of performance.
- Coaches answer the tellers' questions and concerns.
- Coaches take advantage of teachable moments when the group can learn from a student's performance.
- Coaches encourage light moments. The session should be enjoyable and a celebration of each story and each tradition.
- Coaches learn from the students, whose points of view may be entirely original and lend unexpected insight. Listening to them carefully helps to improve and develop everyone's appreciation skills.

7. **Closing Exercise** (approximately 15 minutes)

The last part of the day brings everyone together for closure. During this time:

- Students and coaches discuss what they did in small group.
- If there has been a guest, students and coaches may offer appreciations.

---

*Please note: On days when a guest speaker has been scheduled, the Large and Small Group Coaching times are shortened, and the Small Group Coaching comes right after the Large Group Coaching and before the snack. The guest is always invited ahead of time to join the snack break. (See Table 1.)

- Coaches may ask a student to tell his or her story if the student has a performance coming up or needs the feedback of a larger group.
- A student may tell another student's story to the group, first securing the original teller's permission. The purpose is to give the original teller insight into what listeners are taking away from his or her telling. If it's a personal story, it can be a wonderful way to gain empathy, as Noa Baum points out in chapter 8. The first time this is done, a coach models the activity.
- Students take time to put any closing thoughts into their journals.
- Each member of the group shares one thing they have learned or enjoyed from the activities of the day.

A Glimpse into C@W: *Hero Worship*

A new student had a very obvious case of hero worship for an older, more experienced teller. The older boy had a very distinctive style. Once, at the end of a session, well into the coaching season, we had some extra time. The staff asked the older boy to entertain the group with his story. The younger boy raised his hand and shyly asked if he could tell the older boy's story. The older student agreed. For the next 10 minutes the hero worshiper had us all in hysterics with his caricaturist imitation of his idol. When the laughing died down and eyes were wiped, the older student congratulated the younger one on his performance and said he had even learned a few techniques for his own telling. The staff has since incorporated the practice of sharing each other's stories into each training session.

—Nancy Marie Payne

8. **Reflection** (approximately 3 minutes)

In the first couple of weeks, a coach offers a closing reflection or prayer, the source of which is identified for educational purposes.

For the rest of the season, one of the students volunteers for or is assigned this responsibility on a week-to-week basis. The reading can be a text that has moved them, something from their tradition, or an original thought or prayer. The text may be spoken, sung or chanted. This reflection is intended as an expression of thankfulness for being together and for learning together.

Table 1: Sample C@W Coaching Schedules

No Guest Speaker 2:00–4:30 pm	30-minute Guest Speaker 2:00–4:30 pm	50-minute Guest Speaker 2:00–4:30 pm
Reflection (approx. 3 min.)	**Reflection** (approx. 3 min.)	**Reflection** (approx. 3 min.)
Announcements & Journals (approx. 10 min.)	**Announcements & Journals** (approx. 7 min.)	**Announcements & Journals** (approx. 7 min.)
Warm-ups (approx. 10 min.)	**Warm-ups** (approx. 7 min.)	**Warm-ups** (approx. 7 min.)
Large-Group Coaching (approx. 20 min.)	**Large-Group Coaching** (approx. 15 min.)	**Large-Group Coaching** (approx. 10 min.)
Snack (approx. 15 min.)	**Small-Group Coaching** (approx. 50 min.)	**Small-Group Coaching** (approx. 40 min.)
Small-Group Coaching (approx. 60 min.)	**Snack** (approx. 15 min.)	**Snack** (approx. 10 min.)
	Guest Speaker (30 min.)	**Guest Speaker** (50 min.)
Closing Exercise (approx. 15 min.)	**Closing Exercise** (approx. 10 min.)	**Closing Exercise** (approx. 10 min.)
Reflection (approx. 3 min.)	**Reflection** (approx. 3 min.)	**Reflection** (approx. 3 min.)

Endnote

1. Kristin Linklater. 1976. *Freeing the Natural Voice*. New York: Drama Book Specialists.

CHAPTER 4

Fundamentals of Holding C@W Performances

MICKI GROPER, MARY MURPHY, NANCY MARIE PAYNE

The way C@W's end-of-season performances are put together has changed over time as the goals of the performances have evolved. In the first year, the performance was presented as a recital, giving each brand-new storyteller a chance to tell his or her story to a community audience. For continued growth and support of the program, it became clear that the performance should become a concise display of talent—both new and seasoned—as a showcase for the program.

On the coaching end, this has been addressed by broadening the array of stories told, tightening them up, and keeping an eye on the length of each story. In performance, the storytelling time does not exceed an hour and a half, all told. The C@W performances now present with pride the most enjoyable programs possible.

In a given year, the number of students and their level of experience also impact the way the performances are organized. Now, at the end of the season, each student is still given the opportunity to tell his or her story, either in a large performance or in a smaller story-circle setting.

The Role of Interns

At first, working with a small group of inexperienced students, the coaches and the director created the lineup for the one final performance at the end of the season. As the program grew, the Interfaith Story Circle asked C@W to take over its April meeting. The seasoned interns emceed and told their stories at the (less formal) circle meeting on a weeknight, while the newer students gave a story performance in a theatre-like setting.

It made more sense the following year to have the interns take over the big performance. The newer students told their stories in the relaxed environment of the story circle.

Some years, the coaches decide to put the interns in charge of organizing one or both of the performances. The coaches then share with them the performance goals, which guide their decisions. A coach stands by to monitor and help. Here's the way the interns go about organizing the performances:

- Each student creates a list of the stories in his or her repertoire.
- A group leader and emcee is chosen for each of the two programs (story circle and large performance).
- They decide who will be telling which of their stories and in what order.

The interns enjoy being given the responsibility, and they benefit from the increased experience. It's a natural progression in learning to express themselves and take ownership.

Where Are "Dress Rehearsals" Held?

The director arranges for the group to go into Sunday school classrooms (third grade and up) the week before the final performance so that all students can rehearse their stories in new settings, which have included a Hindu temple, a Turkish cultural center, and a number of churches and synagogues. These rehearsals before ready-made audiences usually work out well.

The group usually meets right after the rehearsal for an hour and a half or so to debrief, eat lunch together, and go over such things as relaxing before the performance, and appropriate attire and conduct.

Where Are Final Performances Held?

Final performances have been held in churches, synagogues, a Hindu temple, a mosque, and a couple of delightful small theatres. Acoustics, line of sight, proximity to audience, handicapped accessibility, general accessibility, and affordability are all important considerations. Many wonderful spaces have been offered free of charge, though most require liability insurance. If there's to be a potluck supper, kitchen access and tables and chairs or picnic tables are needed. Efforts are always made to invite members of the host organization to the event.

A Performance Ritual

C@W coaches have a ritual to begin and end group performances, using the universal symbol of fire to set the storytelling time apart. You're invited to borrow the following ritual, change it to fit your needs, or create your own:

- Before the ritual, the performers are each given a small candle.
- The ritual starts with the emcee lighting one large candle, which has a settling effect on the audience.

- The emcee then says a few words to explain: "The light of this candle represents how stories enlighten us all. Each performer today will have a story from his or her family, culture, or religion. When they join me they will carry an unlit candle representing their story. They will each light their candle from this large candle to show we are united by our stories."
- The performers walk one by one to the large candle, which has been placed on an aluminum tray. They take turns lighting their small candles from the larger candle and then standing their candles alongside the larger candle.
- The emcee then opens the performance.
- At the end of the performance, the emcee extinguishes all the candles and may say some closing words.

The ritual is practiced with the students ahead of time. At one venue a couple of years ago, flames weren't permitted so battery-operated candles were used. They were pretty nice!

> *Stories are light. Light is precious in a world so dark. Begin at the beginning. Tell … a story. Make some light.*
>
> —Kate DiCamillo[1]

Some Further Thoughts

- Name a Stage Manager for each performance to ensure there is one go-to person who knows what is supposed to happen next at every point.
- Publicize the event widely ahead of time. Storytellers enjoy appearing on radio programs or on Community Access TV, and they benefit, too. Free publicity in newspapers, online, etc., is best. Use social media wisely, and enlist the students' help with it!
- Quarter-page black-and-white flyers for the event are inexpensive and easy to hand out and post.
- C@W does not charge admission to performances, but donations are gladly accepted. Have a person or two in charge of collecting donations (or admission, if you decide on charging).
- Volunteers can handle much of the work that needs to be done, with guidance.
- Use a checklist to keep track of what needs to be done (see the appendix).
- At least a month before the event, start working on a paper program to hand out at the performance. If you're going to sell ad space in the program, start that months ahead!
- Consider audio needs and recording options.
- Make sure you have some photographers and videographers to document the event. Discuss with them ahead of time what you'd like them to capture, and talk with them about limiting the use of flash during the performance.

- The large C@W performance is usually followed by an interfaith mixer activity such as the Human Treasure Hunt (see the appendix) and an international vegetarian potluck meal with audience members invited. Be sure to ask for volunteers to organize the meal, buy paper products, provide decorations for the tables, and help in the kitchen and with cleanup.
- Afterwards, thank-you cards to hosts, volunteers, and others who have helped are a very nice touch!

Endnote

1. Kate DiCamillo. 2003. *The Tale of Despereaux: Being the Story of a Mouse, a Princess, Some Soup, and a Spool of Thread*. Cambridge, Mass.: Candlewick Press.

CHAPTER 5

Coaching Tellers to Be Their Unique Selves

MARNI GILLARD

Storytellers of every age need coaching that assists them in developing their creative vision for each tale and for a body of work. The best coaching helps tellers find their unique, authentic approach as they learn common strategies for connecting themselves and their listeners to a story's truth. New tellers need help recognizing and valuing their natural strengths as performers, which can differ widely. Appreciated for and supported in performance strategies that they (often unconsciously) already employ, developing performing artists will find the courage to experiment with new strategies as their awareness and confidence grow.

Coaching differs from theatre directing. A true coach begins by noticing and naming for the developing artist strategies, skills, and stylistic aspects he or she already uses well. New tellers are typically unconscious of what they do intuitively. A second level of coaching comes from non-critical questioning that nudges the teller to examine his or her artistic choices. The myriad choices tale-telling involves include both conscious and unconscious decisions. Such inviting questions as "Tell me more about _____" or "What was happening for you during that moment?" help tellers grow in awareness of how they are leading listeners to meaning. The coach encourages the teller's awareness and self-direction through this appreciative naming of what already works and the kind of questioning that stimulates the teller's imagining of what's possible. The coach uses his or her intelligence to awaken the creative intelligence of the burgeoning artist.

Five Keys of Storytelling Coaching

The following points are adapted from the writings and workshops of Doug Lipman.[1]

1. **BELIEVE in every teller's potential.** Commit to watching for and focusing on a teller's natural strengths. Believe in the artistry ready to be awakened. Success is unique for each teller.

2. **LISTEN from a relaxed, valuing stance.** A listening coach doesn't interrupt or give suggestions when a tale is new. Advice has its place eventually, but growth begins with delighted receiving. "You did that! Well done!" quiets anxiety and builds the desire to improve. Pointed appreciations teach, and gently offered curiosity-based questions (see point 4) come from good listening. They open the teller's thinking. "How was that?" "What did you notice?" "What image or moment felt good?" "Any new insight?" Tellers need practice owning their tales. If repeatedly invited, they will name new understandings and step inside the tale to witness their work. Good listening and the coaching that follows it take time. Both build confidence and artistic consciousness.

3. **APPRECIATE specifically and globally.** Coaches and peer listeners should notice and share what worked. Specific appreciations address word choice, tone, pace, gesture, surprises, or anything satisfying. Naming specific appreciations alerts all who are listening to the countless hows of successful storytelling. "Great pause there—you gave us time to imagine." "That moment (phrase, facial expression, movement, etc.) grabbed me!" "That was an authentic mom tone of voice!" "Cool sound effect." Global appreciations speak to the whole of the telling: "You did it!" "Wow."

   Both kinds of appreciations are important and should be offered one at a time to avoid overwhelming tellers who must make sense of the feedback. If praise seems difficult, an appreciator is stuck in ingrained critic mode, a common trap. Simply release the critic and return to the practices of believing and listening. The practice of appreciating strengths will become a welcome new habit.

   By naming specific strengths, you point to skills. Everyone listening can note the many ways to be successful. The coach can echo a noteworthy appreciation because it is for every teller's benefit. Watch for the receiver's nonverbal responses. Clarify to help him or her take the comment in as a strength. Well-offered appreciations set fire to the artist's mind. "You liked that? Oh, I've got more of that."

   Separate them from questions and suggestions. Ban the comment, "I liked ___, but … ," which counteracts the purpose of giving appreciations.

   What is appreciated by some listeners might not seem like a strength to a coach. Rather than contradict a comment, offer a later lesson on why some word, movement, or sound effect choices work better artistically than others. That prevents the teller and the one who offered the comment from being robbed of practice in giving appreciations.

4. **QUESTION from the desire to understand a teller's choices.** Good questions make good thinkers and don't sound like criticisms. Questions remind tellers that they are crafters of their work. Question sparingly. Lead the teller to evaluate just one or, at most, a few issues.

   Some questions to ask before the telling might be:
   - What's your goal (vision, purpose) in this coaching session?
   - What help are you looking for?

- Would you like us to listen/watch for anything specific?
- Is there a problem to solve?

Many kinds of questions will arrive after a telling, but appreciations must always precede questions. When bringing the appreciation phase to a close, you may ask, "Would you like to hear some questions about your telling?" Again, keep the teller in charge. Questions should come from artistic curiosity; and they will teach curiosity, along with awareness of the many and often unconscious choices that tellers make as they perform.

One kind of question focuses on the Most Important Thing. An MIT question asks a teller to name the essence, focus, or purpose of a tale. Choose one MIT that fits your concern:

- What do you love about this story?
- What matters in this tale?
- What do you want listeners to get?
- Why this story of all of the stories you could tell?

Asked after the telling, when it's clear in the teller's mind, the MIT is reachable. Notice and appreciate the teller's thinking. The MIT is a light that will guide the teller's re-visions.

Good questions point tellers toward their work. Here are some MIT questions to use sparingly and only when they are relevant:

- Did you notice when you truly entered the tale?
- When did you connect to the audience?
- Did any listener reaction affect your telling?
- How might you get to know each character better?
- Do you speak from any one character more easily than others?
- Can you map the geography of your tale?
- Is there a clear narrator voice?
- What did you discover in this telling?
- When are you experiencing the scene versus simply telling what happened?

A great general question is: "What more can you tell me about _____?" Ask without judgment. Encourage the desire to explore or revise with gentle nudges: "I'm curious about _____." "Tell me about the story's pace." "Tell me more about the moment when _____." Tellers will develop a sense of inquiry. Good questions encourage that.

Deep listening, genuine appreciation, and thoughtful questions provide most of what tellers need to grow. Yet a good suggestion, when offered at the right time, can be a powerful teaching tool.

5. **SUGGEST with a light touch.** If it makes sense for a teller, after appreciations and questions, ask, "Would you like a suggestion?" Remind tellers they are in charge—they may be filled with new ideas after appreciations or questions and don't want more ideas just then. Honor that. Beware of suggestions that carry a critical or "fix this" tone.

Watch how tellers take suggestions in. Too much direction can discourage problem-solving. It also turns performers into "pleasers."

Suggestions should offer strategies: "Want to try something?" Offer practices such as playing with a character's voice, physically placing individual characters for conversation, or setting up a stage geography of the scene. Suggestions and questions often point to a teller's need for more information about the text or more dramatic skill for delivery. Successful coaching energizes performers.

Three Coaching Tools

Here are suggestions a coach can offer to help tellers truly understand their stories and engage with themselves and their audience:

1. **CONNECT to the story while learning it.** To know and befriend your story, you must explore it. Story learning is rarely about knowing words or phrases, even though some lines, such as "I'll huff and I'll puff and I'll blow your house down," are learned so they can be repeated and become memorable for listeners. Storytelling is about entering a story's world, characters, and emotions as you imagine them.

   Here are some ways to explore your story:
   - Draw a map of the scenes or characters.
   - Dance your way through scenes.
   - Improvise a co-telling with a friend.
   - Make a list or outline of the key scenes or images.
   - Try telling the tale in five sentences, three sentences, and one sentence.
   - Start telling in a place other than the chronological beginning.
   - Tell from another character's point of view.

   The more you explore playfully, the more the story will get inside you and the more it will open its meanings to you. Stories have layers of meaning. Keep the story fresh for each audience. A story you tell too often can get stale. Never go on automatic pilot and find yourself just recounting a tale without feeling it. That can happen. If you're bored with a story, play with it in new ways or just find a new one to tell.

   To practice, tell your tale aloud, without stopping. If you mess up, just keep going. Getting to the end is important. It's OK to summarize some parts while practicing, but enter the story to see each scene and speak from each character. If you have done this during practice, the audience will come in with you when you are before them.

   Then practice telling to a human. Rehearsing too much with a doll, action figure, or pet as your listener, or practicing alone to walls and mirrors will keep you from learning how to receive audience response. All performers need practice connecting to the smiles, frowns, and looks of confusion or dismay that will come their way. When you see satisfied, delighted looks, watch those faces to build your confidence! Real live listeners subtly co-create with you because they see the tale inside their heads and feel its emotions. They interact with you, even if you are the only one talking.

After you practice with one listener or a small group, ask for appreciations. Hear what they liked. That helps you know the story works! Ask what they saw or felt at certain moments or if anything was confusing. Stories get better when we learn from our listeners. One teller I know asks, "What do you want more of? What do you want less of?" He considers the answers, and makes changes not to please everyone but to tell more skillfully. You can ask friends to interview you about your story's characters, scenes, and details. You'll get good ideas as you respond.

Don't forget to ask yourself: Why am I telling this? What's important to me in this tale? Does every part relate to the MIT? Am I starting and ending confidently? Is it too short? Too long? How can I climb inside the tale's sensory details so the audience can enter as well?

2. **CONNECT to your listeners while you are telling.** Look at them and surf their nods, smiles, and reactions. Invite them with your eyes and your energy to enter the tale with you. Occasionally surprise them by moving close or changing the volume or pace. Lure them in or sometimes pull back your energy. These are all ways to vary but maintain your connection. The audience will follow you. Don't overact, but do use dramatic effects! Each audience will offer you cues about they want or need. Trust your listeners, but nudge them energetically. Use pauses well to allow listeners time to imagine. Breathe. Gradually come to the end so they can take in that the story is over. Never rush off. Generally, avoid scaring or startling the audience, unless you are telling a "jump tale," one constructed for that purpose. Enjoy your applause. Smile and nod or bow before you exit.

3. **CONNECT to yourself by warming up, centering, breathing, drinking water.** Notice your performing space. Where will your gestures and eyes place the characters? Can you sense the narrator in you? When you are ready to start telling, trust yourself and notice your listeners. Walk the world of the tale. Don't worry about mistakes, just keep going. Stay in your story and trust it to hand you what's important to say. Enjoy the creation of your tale, each time.

Endnote

1. Doug Lipman. 1995. The Storytelling Coach: How to Listen, Praise, and Bring out People's Best. Little Rock, Ark.: August House.

_____. 1999. *Improving Your Storytelling: Beyond the Basics for All Who Tell Stories in Work or Play.* Little Rock, Ark.: August House.

_____. 1999. storydynamics.com

_____. 1999. www.facebook.com/douglipman

CHAPTER 6

Constructing Personal Narrative

NORAH DOOLEY

What happened after you left the party, or during the game, or before the big meet, or at the concert, or backstage at the play? These are some of the personal-narrative stories we tell. Was there a moment or incident that caused you to realize that you were different or the same as others? When were you aware of your own power, vulnerability, or identity as you see yourself or as others see you? These are your stories, and who you are is made up of these narratives.

Our human lives are stories. On some level that may sound cheesy or trite, but it is so very real. Our time on the planet has one long narrative arc—from birth to death, from beginning to end. Every day that we are alive mimics that arc in miniature, from waking to sleeping. Even in our slumber our mind creates stories. That said, besides birth and death, there are no pre-established beginnings or endings to a personal story. When we construct a story, we decide on a place to start telling and then a place to end. But the story goes on…

The material of personal stories is all round us. We are made of it. We create stories for every experience. Some are super-short stories that just connect cause and effect and lack any artful touch. Other stories are epics: hilarious or poignant, shallow or deep. We are steeped in stories, think in stories, and live in stories. Stories are how we order and understand our conscious life. They are not just one of many art forms but are how human beings think!

What happened on your weekend, how an historical event impacted you, any human-development milestone (first step, lost tooth, puberty) in your life—these are all stories we tell ourselves. When we share these stories, we share our common humanity as well.

American novelist Kurt Vonnegut had some great advice to writers that I think is helpful for storytellers of personal narrative as well.

[1]His words are in **bold,** and my commentary follows:

1. **Find a subject you care about!** To tell the story well, you will need to practice it over and over again. If you don't care, you'll get bored.

2. **Don't ramble**. Finding the "main thing" and knowing why you are telling a story help you keep on track. Nothing loses an audience faster than a storyteller who wanders.

3. **Keep it simple**. Flowery language or complicated metaphors and sentences are best in writing. Verbal communication will be beautiful and engaging when the teller uses genuine speech and clear language.

4. **Have the guts to cut or take things out.** Sometimes we have a fun or clever way to say something that we love, but it doesn't fit or distracts from the main point. Don't be sad about leaving such things out; they may belong in a poem or an essay or some other piece of your writing.

5. **Sound like yourself.** Don't try to imitate writers, peers, teachers, or speakers you admire. When you are expressing your experience with every part of you, your performance will have enormous power. When any part of your energy is used to imitate or wasted on pretense, you lose power and can distract your audience.

6. **Say what you mean to say.** This goes back to the no-rambling warning and the very first tip to pick something you care about.

7. **Respect your listeners (Vonnegut actually wrote "Pity your readers").** Don't waste their time with trivial nonsense. Self-deprecation can work, but never put your listeners down or go for a cheap laugh. Performance is not talking to your best friend, your mom, or a counselor. In the privacy of such a conversation, it is appropriate for the listener to work to understand you and support you to express yourself. In a performance, speaking your words will help you enormously, but a publicly told story is for the listeners.

Here are some of my suggestions for the ingredients of a good personal-narrative story:

- A good story needs a connection to your personal history and who you are. If you care about it, so will we.
- A good oral story is told from the memory of the experience, not from a set of memorized words.
- A good story needs something to happen. It doesn't necessarily have to be conflict, but something should change, and the change should be significant to you.
- A good story needs strong images and clear words to describe them. No need to get fancy.
- A good story needs active, respectful listeners. Your story comes to life in the act of telling.

You must know why you want to tell this story—or, at the very least, know what truth you want to find in telling the story. I'm not talking about the facts but the meaning you hope to share with listeners. The story should have a question or some insight or truth that makes it worthwhile for the audience to stop, think, and listen. It needn't be something novel. In fact, listeners seem to prefer the familiar.

Arundhati Roy writes:

> … *the secret of the Great Stories is that they have no secrets. The Great Stories are the ones you have heard and want to hear again. The ones you can enter anywhere and inhabit comfortably. They don't deceive you with thrills and trick endings … They are as familiar as the house you live in … You know how they end, yet you listen as though you don't … In the Great Stories you know who lives, who dies, who finds love, who doesn't. And yet you want to know again. That is their mystery and their magic.*[2]

How to Coach Students to Create Personal-Narrative Stories

Start from Their Experiences

Encourage your students to start working on stories from their experiences. Have them get back to the raw material. Instead of recalling the plot and the chain of consequences that links it together, help them remember their sensory experiences of there and then.

As Annie Dillard says:

> *Always locate the reader in time and space again and again. [Do not] rush in to feelings, to interior lives. Instead, stick to surface appearances; hit the five senses; give the history of the person and the place, and the look of the person and the place.… Don't describe feelings. The way to a [listener's] emotions is, oddly enough, through the senses.*[3]

After students have engaged memory and imagination, help them deliberately use their five senses to find details and fully articulate answers to these "W" questions: Where? When? Who? Have them create those answers by thinking, remembering, and imagining. Then, each story needs to answer "What happened?" and tell how it all turns out. The question of "Why tell it?" should be answered by the story itself. Listeners will understand "Why?" from the artful way sensory details, factual information, and nonverbal elements have been mixed.

Structure

A story needs a beginning, a purposeful middle, and a clear ending. An unscripted and spoken narrative needs clear boundaries to keep its form. A beginning place can be imagined from any or a combination of the five senses. A start can be made right in the middle of the action. Often, the middle will take care of itself because it is the exposition, but there must be a clear ending place. Otherwise, the spoken and ephemeral story will be just so much hot air for listeners. They may be entertained, but when the story is over they will not remember what entertained them. A very simple but effective plot form is:

39

1. Establish normal.
2. Something happens.
3. Show the new normal (a direct result of 1 + 2).

Plot is how you arrange the events of your experience to tell your story. Tell us only what we need to know for your story to make sense, and leave out the rest. The oft-taught five-scene plot structure (see Figure 1) may help you refine and decide the elements of your story. The exposition should be very short. It reveals the characters and the setting. Try to get into that rising action right away and have the events become complicated ASAP. During the climax—the turning point or some point of change in your story—you impart new information or understanding from the experience, come to terms with this information, or act on or in this new reality. Events are resolved, and consequences described or understood in the crisis. The denouement is the final outcome or untangling of events in the story.

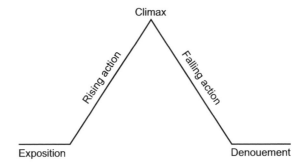

Figure 1: Five-scene plot structure.[4]

Dialogue

Use dialogue to dig deeper. Everyone who talks in a story will reveal who they are, what they feel, how they think, and more. Even if tellers do not use character voices, the words characters say can show us deep meaning worth a novel's worth of words.

Endnotes

1. Kurt Vonnegut, "How to Write with Style," http://peterstekel.com/PDF-HTML/Kurt%20Vonnegut%20advice%20to%20writers.htm.
2. Arundhati Roy. 1998. *God of Small Things*. First HarperPerennial edition.
3. Annie Dillard, "Notes for Young Writers," in *Lessons in Persuasion*, Lee Gutkind (Pittsburgh, Penn.: University of Pittsburgh Press, 2000).
4. Freytag's Pyramid, Wikipedia (public domain).

CHAPTER 7

The Special Use of Folktales

LAURA SIMMS

It is time for us to recognize the power of the folktale experience. A folktale breathed into life through the living presence and reciprocity of a storyteller has advantages often overlooked. We have been trained to use folktales the way an actor uses scripts, assuming that the words and content are the tale or that what is most significant is the lesson being presented. But the real wealth of the folktale is released in the dynamic experience of the unfolding engagement where the listener becomes the story, moment by moment, through the multidimensional imaginative and emotional response it engenders.

There is a Tibetan proverb that says that teaching concepts or making interpretations (for instance, summing up a story with a moral attached at the end as the main point) is like training someone who has no legs to walk. What distinguishes engaged storytelling from more passive forms of narrative is the way in which listeners, drawn out of self-preoccupation, co-create the story. The experience of engagement enlivens from head to toe and sometimes grows new legs.

In 2013, I had a grant from a special project at Rutgers University in Newark, New Jersey, to work with a local health initiative. Part of the program placed me in an after-school classroom in a violent neighborhood. In one school, I had told an Inuit story of The Girl Who Married a Ghost. A chief on an island, inspired by greed, refused to marry his youngest daughter to any suitor unless he was offered a high "bride price." Late one night, a stranger arrived with unlimited wealth. The chief married his daughter to him in the middle of the night without question. What he did not know was that he had married his daughter to the Chief of Ghosts and sent her to live in the Land of the Dead. The story explains her discovery of a daytime land of skeletons and ruins. Her attempt to escape was futile and she eventually became accustomed to the laws of that land relayed to her by a half woman, half Screech Owl. In the end, she was returned to our world with a son and given conditions for his becoming a human child. She failed and had to return to the Land of the Dead. She and the child became ghosts and found peace in that world, but the path between worlds has disappeared, except for Screech Owl woman, who still flies back and forth and terrifies us at night.

Everyone fell into the story. Afterwards they created huge drawings of demons, monsters, ghosts, and invented hybrid characters. All embodied dangers that they imagined and that they experienced in their daily lives. Then each person located and drew a heart, small or large, in each drawing and created stories about how to transform the creatures.

On the second day, we shared those stories and talked about what it had been like to listen to the story. An argument broke loose, like a sudden tidal wave, during our conversation. It was between a boy who had been in the school all year and a young African girl who had been brought to Newark from West Africa after the brutal murder of her mother two weeks before. Because we were in the container of listening and dialogue, drenched in the images of the story, we were able to process this argument by talking about the unfamiliar way that Inuit People talked about ghosts. I turned the conversation toward a reflection about death and rituals in different cultures. The African girl was able to explain to all of us how her aunt, who she now lived with, believed in ghosts, especially those whose death was sudden and violent. The boy, hearing her story, without our blaming him, calmed down enough to recognize that he had no idea about her life or upbringing and beliefs. In the end, he apologized and said that he had hated hearing her speak about her mother because it made him sad.

It was a very powerful afternoon. We ended by drawing islands, at the suggestion of another girl. "You can put anything you want on your islands," I said, and most everyone focused into the large empty white paper and began the dreamlike endeavor of making an island of their own creation.

I left feeling we had made progress. After all, this was a violence-prevention program that promoted mindfulness and storytelling. The mission was to offer visceral tools so the children could become familiar with their own capacity to rest their mind—and sustain the emotions roused in a roomful of people, without having to react against oneself or another.

But the next day proved me wrong. Whatever we had achieved was overwhelmed by the events of the day in the school before my arrival. The kids sat as if they were hardened into shock or outrage. They did not acknowledge me when I entered the room. I felt as if they were protecting themselves in an inarticulate disconnection. As I sat down on a table at the front of the room, they resorted to patois chatter in languages of origin, or tossing things off their desks. A teacher, who had been seated in the back of the room marking papers, came forward and told me it was the result of a bully whose need to enjoy someone else's misery had rattled the entire school. "He was wielding a gun after lunch, in three classrooms." Their sorrow, finding no outlet in conversation or time to process, was now disguised as rage against themselves and others.

One girl became the victim of a spontaneous fight. She tightened her lips and crossed her arms. There was little I thought I could do directly. So I acknowledged that the room felt really intense. I asked if they wanted to talk about anything. They said, unanimously, "No." So I said, "Okay. I will tell stories, and if you want to listen, you can. If you want to draw, you can. If you want to space out, you can do that as well." I told three stories. Back to back. I felt like a woman in a boat meant for 20, paddling continuously to keep us from drowning. In our two hours, those who listened, listened. Perhaps we repaired torn internal stitches by listening to stories with structure and irresistible images. Some kids drew. I never scolded anyone. Only once I said, "It is all right if you don't want to listen, but you can go to the back of the room if you can't help but disturb others. I can see you are really full of a lot of feelings." And a boy walked to the back of the room.

Suddenly he called out, "Hey. What about that story you told us the other day about the girl who married a ghost?" I turned on my tape recorder and began the story. I asked them if they could be the soundscape. They could use their voices in any way they wanted and I would play it back, I told them. It was a bit chaotic at first. I said, "You know the story, so you can make the music the way it is in a film. When danger is about to come, the sound starts." I began the story; they made a buzzing noise. "That is great," I said. And then they continued. Violent episodes, hidden cemeteries, weapons—all were spiced into the story. Each time someone yelled out, I tucked it into the story as if there were worlds beneath the sea, dreams that some people had, and events that occurred that had not been in the original story.

They sent out their distressed voices with passion, becoming a communal soundscape that brought wind and sea, danger, anger, fear, footsteps, and ghosts singing to life. The passion of engagement was forceful. When the story was not violent enough to match the state of mind of one or another, they added sections like "Under that tent was a graveyard with skeletons yelling" and "A monster killed someone and they were bad." We were sewing up shredded confidence as we invented creatures—zombies, demons, or weird ordinary people—who had lost their hearts.

This litany of energetic descriptions gave voice to feelings without invasion or explanation, or to frustration without personal attack. Through this elaborate quest into the dark, we found light. They transformed creatures into helpers who nursed soul and spirit. I think they were becoming cosmic street cleaners, all seeing flying angels and agents of beauty appearing out of the tumult of the story and the tumult of their own experience that had no words at the start of the class. At the end of two hours, we listened back to the soundscape. The story—which was about deceit, violence, death, and fear—provided something larger than the opened wound they felt to guide us back to the island sanctuary where the girl and her child could find peace of mind.

The folktale telling can be a way of providing space for feelings and energy that are not expressed constructively anywhere or in any way in children's daily lives. I had the sense in Newark that if anyone came into the room while we were making the CD of this ghost story, they would think I was promoting violence. Yet the communal story seemed to hold the energy and transform it on the spot into something else. It gave them access to natural imaginative emotional responses, while bringing their stressed minds back into the body of listening where nerve endings, cut off and not used, are restored into action.

A written story is not a script. When the storyteller takes the time to become aware of what is taking place in the story in an obvious way, in a psychological way, and also on the visceral level of engaged listening, then the folktale becomes a constantly giving gift. It can restore dignity, attention, and a capacity to listen and reflect with an open heart in need of a place to beat and feel and express.

Earlier tellers realized that to listen was to be in the story and that each tale offered multiple experiences which reshaped and opened the mind. Unlike the fairy tale, which journeys between worlds and tracks the initiation of a hero or heroine whose bravery or kindness will rebalance what has been out of order in the world, the folktale is perfect for exploring daily issues. The listener can project his or her imagination onto the story unfolding, without having to be triggered by personal trauma, paralyzing issues, or shame. It makes each listener capable of reflecting on difficult issues, because the telling itself has detachment, intimacy of listening, and a key to unlocking an individual's ability to think about both sides of a situation without having to assign blame or inflame bias. Recently I experienced this when I introduced the following Indian folktale to a group of Junior High School students:

The Mice and the Elephant

Once upon a time there was a colony of mice who lived in a forest. Whenever the elephants walked through their land with their enormous feet, many of the little creatures were harmed. One day, the mouse king went to the King of the Elephants. He scrambled up the elephant's trunk and whispered into his ear, "If you spare our lives, we will help you in a time of need." The elephant king was sensitive and wise. He took pity on the small animals to whom he had never paid attention and agreed. That day he ordered the elephants to be careful and never step on a single mouse.

From that day forth the elephants were attentive as they walked. They lifted their huge legs carefully, never harming their tiny friends. When they entered the land of the mice, they lifted their trunks and trumpeted a warning to their small friends, "We are walking. We are walking." The mice answered, "We are walking. We are walking."

Both creatures lived more happily. As they became aware of one another, their eyes and ears grew sharper to what was around them, and their hearts grew more loving.

One day, elephant trappers came to the forest. They were capturing elephants for a human king's soldiers to ride into battle. Day by day more and more elephants were caught in great rope traps and bound to large trees so that they could be taken away.

The elephant king was very sad. Then he remembered the promise of the mouse king. He called for his friend. The tiny king arrived and listened to the elephant's story.

Immediately, the mouse king called all the mice together. Thousands and thousands of mice gathered from every direction to discuss how they might help the elephants. No one had forgotten how their huge friends spared their lives. No one had forgotten how the voices of the elephants had called out to them in the forest. One clever mouse suggested a plan. All the mice rejoiced.

That evening they formed into little groups. Each group gnawed the ropes of a single trap with their tiny sharp teeth. They worked all night. They never rested, and by morning all the elephants were freed. The forest exploded with the joyful sounds of elephants and mice in celebration.

Frustrated, the trappers left the forest.

The elephant king was grateful. He lifted the little mouse king on his back and decreed, "From today onwards elephants and mice will be the best of friends." And to this day, that is the truth. The elephants and the mice are still good friends. Regardless of their differences in size, they saved each other's lives.

I said that a tale of this sort would be told not only to children but to people of all ages, because it was worthy of contemplation. After telling it, I asked, "What does this remind you of in your own lives?" They talked about bullying and about fear. Someone talked about feeling limited and imprisoned by rules that were unjust. Because the story was short, I told it a second time as a call and response event, saying, "Perhaps we can now look at the depth of possible emotions inside the story."

I said one sentence and had the group repeat it. When I was the elephant, I asked for the feeling of the elephant at the start of the tale, in the middle, and at the end. A deep voice, mindless and confident, was the first. A slower and more relaxed deep voice occurred in the middle and at the end, when imprisoned in a rope trap. Their voices were harsh and full of agony. The mice had smaller voices.

The same process was repeated. The voice of the storyteller of course was neutral relating events. That did not change. It allowed them to practice moving from strong emotions and situations without getting stuck in either one. It was a covert exercise of learning to sit with feelings and let them go rather than get stuck in them. They went from being victims, to helpers, victorious over situations, to needing help, until at the end all rejoiced. Surprising themselves, the young adults spontaneously said, "And they lived happily ever after." A wiggle of giggles spread through the room as their own childlike wonder escaped.

On another day, we were able to discuss the nature of sharing solutions and depending on each other by talking about elephants and mice so no person was embarrassed or highlighted. We even discussed how the story could have had other outcomes if the elephants refused to pay attention. "What would have happened when the hunters came?" I asked. And they were moved to realize that the huge creatures they had just become would have been hunted and harmed and taken from their natural environment. So much was discovered in this exercise of communal storytelling. I realized it could emphasize the living together in a natural way that is destroyed when greed and lack of respect for others inflict their harm. It served us when we talked about racism and bullying, and it was also fun. Fun to become characters and voices permitting expression.

CHAPTER 8

Storytelling Across Borders: Listening to "the Other"

Noa Baum

An enemy is a person whose story we have not heard.

—Gene Knudsen-Hoffman, Quaker peace activist

I grew up in Jerusalem, Israel. When my grandmother would hear the word "Arab," she would spit and say, "May their name be erased." Her son was killed in the war of 1948.

In 1993, when I lived in California, I met a woman on the playground. I knew she was a Palestinian—I recognized her beauty from home—but I didn't know if she'd want to talk to me. Nonetheless, I went up and asked her what her baby's name was, and we started to talk. Over the years our kids grew up together and were friends. Then, in 2000, I was working on creating a story from my memories of the 1967 war, when I was in third grade, and I realized that for the past seven years I had known this woman who grew up in Jerusalem, not five miles from where I grew up, and I had never really heard what that war was like for her. I became curious and I called her, and a very new chapter in our relationship began: we started to talk intensely. This time I asked questions, and for the first time in my life I heard what it actually felt like to be a Palestinian and live under Israeli occupation.

She told me how when she was 10, she saw a 14-year-old boy being beaten by soldiers and driven away. She said it was the first time she felt hate and understood what that word meant. For me, hearing this was like being hit in the gut. Those soldiers that she hated, that terrified and haunted her entire childhood, were my people, our boys, everyone I knew that turned 18 and went to the army, including my brother! It was hard but I kept listening because she was telling me her story.

We continued to talk. Eventually, we started to talk about our "history," the national narratives that are at the heart of the Israeli-Palestinian conflict. When I mentioned a known fact, what was the truth for me, she would say, "That's not true. That's Zionist propaganda!"

When she told me what was truth for her and what she learned at school as history, I would say, "That's not true at all. That's Arab propaganda!"

This would lead to arguing, but then she would say, "Look at us. We're getting defensive again." We would laugh, and I would pick up the baby so that she could make soft-boiled eggs for the other kids. And we would continue to talk.

We were able to continue talking and listening to each other, in spite of not always agreeing, because we had trust and love between us, because we had heard each other's stories.

It was this very powerful experience that propelled me to create a performance piece based on our conversations, called *A Land Twice Promised*. In it I tell our personal stories that echo the contradictory national narratives of our people. I've been performing it internationally for more than 14 years. I've recently written a book about it, *A Land Twice Promised: An Israeli Woman's Quest for Peace*.

I realized that three things I learned from this process could be useful for anyone dealing with issues of diversity: the way of listening deeply, the way stories allowed us to put aside our judgments and explore our differences in a non-threatening manner, the way telling each other our personal stories actually expanded our ability to accept things that contradicted everything we previously held as truth.

My story is not just about one woman connecting to another. It's not even about an Israeli connecting to a Palestinian. It's about the power of storytelling and the power of listening to the story of "the other," even—in fact, especially—when that other is very different from you and when his or her story may be difficult to hear.

In workshops that I've developed for communities, interfaith groups, colleges, and businesses, participants are invited to share stories and learn to listen to "the other." Unlike when we share opinions and concepts, when we share a story we open up to another person's experience, and something extraordinary happens.

First, Story shifts the emotional connection. In a very short time there's a sense of trust and intimacy. You may not know all the facts about that person, but you feel as if you have a glimpse into his or her world that is larger and deeper than you would have in other encounters.

It is not just the content of the story; it's the process of being in the same space, sharing your experience, listening and being listened to, that creates change.

Second, Story shifts the cognitive connection. We are attached to our thinking, our cognitive constructs of our world, our opinions. But when we listen to someone's story/experience we are using what Annette Simmons calls "the world's oldest form of virtual experience—the imagination."[1] By using the imagination we are able to look at the world in a way that is not ours and thus expand our ability to accept multiple/diverse points of view.

Being able to imagine and understand the point of view of "the other" does not mean you have to adopt it or that it invalidates your older opinion. It just means you can virtually add another experience through your imagination.

Eventually, adding on another's point of view may challenge your opinions, or perhaps it may reveal misconceptions—but you don't have to change or replace them in the moment. It's not a declaration of defeat.

Story allows us to suspend judgment and expand our ability to hold multiple or contradicting points of view or as Maxine Hong Kingston writes, "I learned to make my mind large, as the universe is large, so that there is room for paradoxes."[2] When I listened to my Palestinian friend's stories, I was able to make my mind large, make room for paradox: holding a perception and interpretation that was different and foreign and even threatening to mine.

Simulating the technique I use in my performance piece, participants also learn to tell someone else's story from their point of view. The challenge of not only listening to someone else but telling the story of "the other" can deepen compassion and understanding for both teller and listener.

Storytelling is a powerful tool to create trust, change attitudes, learn about other cultures, and expand our ability to accept differences.

Storytelling Workshop: Listening to "the Other"

To assist you in planning your own storytelling coaching sessions to help students tell their stories and listen to others' stories, here is an outline of a workshop I conduct with students from grades 7 to 12:

Objectives

Students will:

- Experience the power of individual stories to take us beyond rhetoric.
- Develop understanding and tolerance of other cultures.
- Explore connections to their culture.
- Expand their ability to accept differences.
- Enhance their listening and communicating skills.
- Deepen trust of one another and build community.

Lesson Plan

Introduction

I usually use my personal story as a modeling and springboard for the lesson plan. In situations where students have not heard the performance, I talk briefly about the personal experience that inspired the show and explain that in this lesson we will use a model I developed based on what I learned.

I recommend sharing a personal experience as a point of entry to this lesson. Any personal experience that you can share about encountering "the other" will help engage the students and lead into the opening discussion. You may choose to tell about a time when:

- You met someone who was very different from you or was considered "the enemy."
- You met someone who was always one of "them" and discovered you actually had a lot in common.
- You formed an opinion about someone who was different without really knowing much about them, or this happened to someone close to you.
- You were judged or labeled.

Opening Discussion

Lead a discussion with these questions:

- What are the things that make us who we are? (our traditions, families, nationalities, religion, gender)
- What do people fight about?
- Is there a way to claim who we are and let our differences move us closer to peace rather than to fighting? Let's try.

Finding a Story

My instructions to the students go something like this:

1. Close your eyes and think of (choose one):
   - a special celebration in your family
   - a time you were grateful/proud to be part of your heritage/people/tradition
   - a time/event/person that made you feel you belonged to your heritage/people/ tradition
2. Imagine the place where your story begins as if you're watching a movie in your mind's eye. See the details, what things look like. Who else is there?
3. Before sharing your story, here are a few things to remember:
   - Share only what you are comfortable sharing and that it is okay for others to hear.
   - Listen to everyone else's stories with no interruptions.
   - Listen to their stories with delight: show attention with your eyes, face, and body.

Sharing the Story

1. Students partner up and take turns sharing (90 seconds to 2 minutes each).

2. After student A shares a story, give the following instruction: Before we switch, Listener, please give an appreciation (30 seconds):
   - "What I liked about your story was _____."
   - "A moment in your story that was especially vivid was _____."
3. Change roles: student B now shares a story and gets an appreciation.
4. Give the following instruction to the students who told first: Reflect on the story you heard. Turn to your partner and ask a curious question such as, "This _____ interests me. Can you say more about it?" or "I'm curious about _____. Could you tell me more?"
5. Partners answer and then change roles.

Reflection (With Partner or as Entire Class)

Ask the students:

1. How did it feel to tell?
2. How did it feel to listen and be listened to?

Deepening Connections

1. Instruct the students: With a new partner, tell your story again. Note if answering the "curious" question brought up anything for you that needs to be added or taken out of your story.
2. Listener gives an appreciation and then tells his or her story.
3. After each partner tells his or her story, instruct the students: Close your eyes and see the story you heard as a movie in your mind.
4. Partners take turns asking each other questions. Encourage them to get details about feelings, places, other people, and go beyond what things looked or sounded like—find out what they smelled, tasted, or felt like.

Putting Yourself in Someone Else's Shoes

1. Instruct the students: With your partner, join another pair to form a group of four. (Alternatively, the students can tell to the whole class.)
2. Tell your partner's story using the first person ("I"). Make it sound like it happened to you. A few things to keep in mind:
   - Do the best you can to stay true to the truth of the story.
   - Don't imitate your partner's voice.
   - Don't worry about structure or plot. See if you can tell it as if it actually happened to you. Experiment with thoughts and feelings.

51

Group Feedback

Each person gives appreciation. Ask the students:

1. What moments worked?
2. What did you like?

Discussion and Reflection

Ask the students:

1. How did it feel to tell your story to someone?
2. How did it feel to hear your partner retell the story?
3. How did it feel to listen to someone else's story?
4. How did it feel to retell it?
5. How is storytelling different from debating or arguing?

Closing Circle

Each student says, "One thing I'm taking away is _____."

Assessment

Ask students to identify and write about an issue of disagreement or dual perspectives that emerged from their storytelling experience, discussing the differences of viewpoint. Were there any shifts in personal viewpoints? If shifts occurred, explain why; if shifts did not occur, explain why not. Assess the writer's ability to articulate "the other's" point of view, and his or her degree of respect for that viewpoint.

This chapter previously appeared in Social Studies in the Storytelling Classroom, *Jane Stenson and Sherry Norfolk. Little Rock, AR: Parkhurst Brothers.* Copyright 2012 Noa Baum.

Endnotes

1. Annette Simmons. 2006. *The Story Factor.* Cambridge, Mass.: Basic Books.
2. Maxine Hong Kingston. 1975. *The Woman Warrior: Memoirs of Girlhood Among Ghosts.* New York: Vintage.

CHAPTER 9

Uniting Immigrant Voices: Sharing Life Stories and Folktales

BARBARA ALIPRANTIS

It all began that fateful day when I was taken from the small fishing village on the Aegean island of Paros, Greece, where I had been born just two and a half years earlier. I left my beloved village with my mother and my siblings: nine-year-old brother, Yianni, and sister, Calypso, 13 months older than I. Thus began my Greek-American odyssey and my lifelong passion to advocate for fellow immigrants.

I remember the day we left Naoussa as though it were yesterday. The winding labyrinth-like village lanes and alleyways were lined with people, young and old, crying and waving goodbye. Our caravan of donkeys laden with trunks, blankets, and assorted supplies set out for the eight-mile walk to the port of Barkia, where we would board a ferry that would transport us to Piraeus, the port of Athens, where we would board the *Nea Hellas*, which would take us to America. Although I had no idea where we were going, I was a precocious toddler and I smelled trouble in the air. What I did know was what my mother had repeatedly told us for months: "*Paidia* [children], we are going to America to meet your father. He is waiting for us."

When we finally arrived in America, after a long voyage across the Atlantic, my father was there with open arms. A Greek merchant marine, he had been traveling back and forth to America for many years, "jumping ship" from one sea voyage to another, working as a dishwasher in a coffee shop in Astoria, New York, and sending money home to his young family in Paros. With the help of cousins and compatriots, he managed to avoid immigration officials, who were always lurking around looking for "illegals."

Eventually my father returned to Paros. He then reentered the United States legally, sponsored by my mother's first cousin Peter Caparis. After gathering the necessary paperwork, my father sent for us and we went to live with him in Brooklyn, New York.

My Greek-American immigrant childhood played out on the stoops and concrete sidewalks of Brooklyn in a primarily Jewish neighborhood where I learned to embrace diversity as a strength.

Fourteen months after we arrived in this country, my younger sister was born, and our mother died from complications a few days after the birth. Uncle Peter and his young wife opened their home to us and we moved in with them. We were also welcomed by their wonderful neighbors. My experiences living in this welcoming, multiethnic community are part of the reason why I came to love and embrace being different, being Greek.

I entered first grade as a child who did not have a mother, grandparents, or even a reliable command of the English language. The language spoken at home was primarily Greek. The previous year, I had been looking through my older sister's first grade reader, *Dick and Jane*, with its lovely pictures of mothers, fathers, and grandparents—and I wondered why they did not look anything like my family or the village folks I left behind in Greece. I had more than the usual trepidation a new first grader feels.

I remember my teacher calling the roll on that first day of school. Reflecting back on it now, I see that what happened vividly illustrates the words of American author Henry Adams, who wrote in 1918: "A teacher affects eternity … he can never tell where his influence stops."

Miss Pheifer called out the last names of my classmates, one by one, "Aaron, Abraham, Adelman, Agostino –" and then she stopped, unable to pronounce the next name. Looking around the room she asked, "Who's Barbara?" I raised my hand ever so slowly. "How do you say that name?" she asked, spelling it slowly, "A–R–I–A–N–O–U–T–S–O–S. Is that a Greek name?" When I pronounced it for her, her face broke into a big smile, and she said, "Children, Barbara is Greek. *How wonderful*! Barbara, stand up and tell us about yourself."

I loved an audience even then, so I stood up and told them about the dramatic events that unfolded the day I left my beloved Greek island home. In that moment, I became a storyteller; I've been telling and retelling that story ever since, and have added hundreds of other stories to my repertoire. I am forever grateful to the wonderful teachers in Flatbush, Brooklyn, for teaching me to love who I was: a small immigrant child who loved to tell stories about the village folks she left behind; loved sharing her family's teaching tales, including folktales and fables; and loved talking about her Greek-American immigrant experience. I had no way of knowing if, in fact, I was the only immigrant student, but all through grade school each teacher rejoiced in my being the only Greek child in the room. This, too, taught me to love being different, being Greek!

Like many immigrant families, we were encouraged to speak only our native tongue at home, and for many years we had private lessons and learned to read and write it as well. A few years after graduating high school, I married into a Greek-American family who also spoke only Greek at home. This helped me continually maintain and improve my mastery of my native tongue.

Thus, in 1980, I was hired to work as the Resident Storyteller at St. Joseph's School for the Deaf in the Bronx; I was a "bilingual Greek-American storyteller" eager to learn a new language, American Sign Language (ASL). On the job, I first learned Signed Exact English through a modality called Total Communication. Then I learned Pidgin Signed English (PSE) and finally, ASL. Eventually I enrolled at Empire State College (SUNY), designed an interdisciplinary degree for myself, and in 1989 graduated with a BA in the Performing Arts with a concentration in Total Communication and Performance.

As part of my college work, I attended a week-long storytelling workshop intensive at the Omega Institute, facilitated by America's foremost deaf actor Bernard Bragg, co-founder of the National Theatre of the Deaf. There I learned how to tell stories not only with the spoken word but also using Cinematic Sign Language and Visual Vernacular. When signing a story using Cinematic Sign Language, you imagine you are shooting a movie: your eyes are the camera, and your hands make the images. You have to think about long shots, close-ups, and overlays, which are a combination of the two, and you need to be mindful of rhythm, duration of images, and phrasing. Visual Vernacular is a combination of expressive theatrical techniques, plus sign language. It involves using ASL vocabulary, hand gestures, facial expressions, and shifting body placement to convey complex and emotionally loaded images.

In 1989, I left St. Joseph's and took a position as the director of the Library Learning Center at the Lexington School for the Deaf in Jackson Heights, working with high school students. I also began teaching a course I designed, Introduction to Sign Language Communication through Storytelling, in the Continuing Education Department at Queensborough Community College.

A decade later, I left the school setting to become a full-time professional storyteller. I joined the Flushing Jewish Community Council Multicultural Committee, hoping it would open up opportunities to draw on my training as a trilingual (English, Greek, ASL) storytelling/teaching artist to work within the diverse ethnic immigrant communities in the borough of Queens.

One of my first assignments was to facilitate an after-school storytelling series in a middle school, working with six newly arrived immigrants. They were all hearing, but, to varying degrees, they were English language learners. The goal was to help them develop and improve their English skills through storytelling.

Armed with ASL games specifically suited for English language learners, including pantomime (the easiest form of nonverbal communication), as well as the spoken word, I entered the room with little trepidation, great enthusiasm, and an open heart. I was greeted by six 13-year-old boys looking less than thrilled to be there. One young man, however, seemed genuinely pleased to meet me. Grinning from ear to ear, he stood up and introduced himself as Gurwinder Singh, and then went on to say, "You can call me Bob. I'm Punjabi. My friends here do *not* speak English, so I'll be happy to interpret for them."

I told Bob that I, too, was an immigrant. I walked over to the large world map on the wall, pointed to New York City, and spoke, using PSE, which is a combination of ASL, the spoken word, and Manually Coded English (MCE). MCE comprises a variety of visual communication methods expressed through the hands; these methods attempt to represent the English language, and generally follow the grammar of English.

"We are here," I began. And, pointing to my homeland, Greece, "I was born there. Where were you born?" Pointing to a region in India, Bob repeated my question in Punjabi for his classmates. And thus began a fascinating communication dance among English, PSE, and Punjabi. After meeting with me for five weeks, Bob and his classmates wrote, with my help, "A Punjabi Love Story," which is included at the end of this chapter.

In my work with Bob and his friends, I was able to draw on the many years I had spent telling stories to students at St. Joseph's School for the Deaf, and the three years I had worked with high school students at the Lexington School for the Deaf. Many of those students had come from inner-city multilingual hearing immigrant families who did not speak English very well and had no knowledge of sign language. Many of the students were multiply handicapped with special needs. While I was telling stories to these children, I was also listening to *their* stories. I would oftentimes meet with their hearing, non-signing, immigrant parents to help them communicate with their children. Some parents tried to learn sign language, but it was extremely difficult because they were learning English *and* coping with the challenges of raising a deaf child. The parents would turn to the school staff to help them communicate with their children.

I treasure the experience I had working with deaf children and their families because I observed firsthand that by role modeling the oral tradition and sharing my immigration stories—including the death of my mother—I was helping my students, especially the teenagers, open up to me and share their family stories. Those stories could be quite difficult, but they were so much a part of their everyday experience and, therefore, part of them. Many told me I gave them courage to tell their story to me.

Today, years later, I've reconnected with some of my students on Facebook, and they touch my heart when they tell me I was the best teacher they ever had because I listened to them.

Sampler of Interactive Activities for Speakers of Languages Other Than English

The visual accompaniment of natural hand gestures and facial expressions—used by all people—*and* some ASL lexicon adds depth of expression and understanding to any spoken story, for all ages, even for people with perfect hearing.

These playful activities illustrate the importance of *visual awareness*—that is, facial expression and body language when communicating in any language other than one's mother tongue. They are especially effective for adolescents and teenagers because they inspire confidence, bond the group, and, above all else, create a safe environment for creative expression.

These activities are adapted from the book *Signs for All Seasons*.[1]

Mirror Exercise

Objective: To mimic exactly the motions of another person.

Value: To increase awareness of movement in specific detail.

To play: Two players face one another, standing or sitting. One will be the "mirror," and the other will be the person looking into the mirror. The "mirror" must copy simultaneously all of the actions of the person looking into the mirror, such as combing or brushing their hair, brushing their teeth, or shaving. Then the players switch roles.

Magic Wand

Objective: To mime a variety of actions using a small wooden dowel (or pencil).

Value: To stretch the imagination and increase the ability to perceive basic shapes in a variety of everyday items.

To play: One player takes the dowel and mimes using it as a recognizable object—for example, a baton, baseball bat, tooth pick, or golf club. He or she passes it to the next player, who uses it the same way, then transforms it into something else and passes it on. Play continues until each player has had a turn.

Mime Time

Objective: To act out individual words or phrases.

Value: To increase the ability to think and communicate without words.

Materials needed: A stack of index cards bearing action words, animals, occupations, etc.

To play: Each player selects a card and then mimes the action or item. Play continues until everyone has had a turn.

Endnote

1. Suzie Linton Kirchner. 1981. *Signs for All Seasons: More Sign Language Games*. Northridge, Calif.: Joyce Media, Inc.

A Punjabi Love Story

BY GURWINDER (BOB) SINGH AND CLASSMATES
EDITED BY BARBARA ALIPRANTIS 2004

Once there was a young couple, a handsome boy and a beautiful girl. They were very much in love. Their parents did not approve. Simply stated, they did not want the young couple to see one another, that is to say, "keep company."

The girl's parents and the boy's parents did everything they could to keep them from seeing one another. Somehow the young couple managed to sneak out and meet from time to time.

Everyone was unhappy: the young couple because they knew it was wrong to deceive their parents, yet kept meeting in secret; the parents because they suspected that their children were seeing one another and they did not know what to do about the situation. Many weeks of sadness passed.

After much agonizing the young couple ran away from their parents' city and were married. While they were extremely happy to be married, they were also filled with sadness because no family or friends were present to witness the marriage.

When their parents learned through various sources what the young couple had done, they were heartbroken. The parents sent word to the young couple that they were never to return home.

As the years passed the young couple was blessed with the birth of three beautiful children, two boys and a girl. They welcomed each child with joy and sadness, knowing full well that their children might never know their grandparents.

Finally a day arrived when they found the courage to return to their parents' city to ask forgiveness and introduce them to their grandchildren.

This storyteller is pleased to report that, after many tears and exchange of words, there was a splendid reconciliation. The girl's parents embraced their long-lost daughter, the boy's parents welcomed their son home, and the three lovely grandchildren were welcomed with open arms by both sets of grandparents.

We trust that they all lived happily ever after.

The End

CHAPTER 10

Empower Youth by Letting Go

KEVIN D. CORDI

Writer Hermann Hesse once said, "Some of us think holding on makes us strong; but sometimes it is letting go." Holding tight leaves no room for movement.

When I began coaching my own storytelling guild, the award-winning Voices of Illusion, I held the reins tight. I feared my students would drift away if I didn't organize or orchestrate the group. Over the years, however, I eventually found a more thorough and nuanced approach. I share the journey in this chapter.

How It Began

Sophomore Jennifer Wooley noticed I always told stories in every class I taught. "True, Jennifer," I said, smiling, and shared, "I stopped apologizing for that a long time ago. In fact, stories help people …"

She interrupted me: "No, you don't understand, I enjoy your stories. In fact, I would love to learn more about storytelling. I want to tell stories. I want to be a storyteller. I would like to have a storytelling club. Can we have one?"

I didn't know where to begin. I had heard of Robert Rubinstein's storytelling club in Eugene, Oregon, but had no clue how to build one. Full of enthusiasm, Jennifer assured me she would take care of all the arrangements and had it planned in a week.

Eager for our inaugural meeting, six of us met in a dark, dank basement, ready to tell ghost stories for half an hour. The chills and thrills echoed the room, spilling over to three and a half hours. We shared the joy of children's books and recounted a few tales shared by our grandparents. The clock moved fast but we were spellbound. We wanted more. And sure enough, Jennifer stood and said, "Next week's meeting will be …"

After that, with the help of Jennifer, I structured the meetings, organized the rooms, and made all the calls. I was new at this, but I learned with each experience.

Questions abounded about the group:

- How would I take attendance?
- Why did this person not come to the meeting?

- Why did this person stay?
- Should we wear uniforms?
- How do we begin?

Then we had our first show. We were asked to tell at the Tehachapi Wind Fair, in California. Students who had never been in the library spent excessive time after school searching for folktales about the wind. We copied and shared tales. We haphazardly but seriously prepared. We piled in the van; we did not know where we were going. We had to find better directions. I remember making one student a "keeper of the map," and when he had this role, we found the way. When we arrived, we could not find the person in charge. We had forgotten some of the lunches. There were hulking wind turbines, and we were assigned to tell next to them. The irony is that the wind was so bad few people heard us. I did realize a bigger lesson from that experience: we needed direction. I also learned that I needed to delegate responsibilities.

So, after, when we were invited to tell stories at an area mall, I created the role of Story Manager. It is like a stage manager in theatre, but this person is in charge of all the non-performance duties of making sure we are prepared for each show during the season. We created a Director of Publicity in charge of promoting our upcoming shows. We elected Co-chairs, who helped run the meetings and arranged reminders about the meetings. The Secretary made sure we had agendas and minutes. Each student who wanted to be involved in the management of the group was provided a space and responsibility in the group.

I needed to deeply listen to my students' needs and change our direction based on the needs.

Selecting Stories

Students should tell the stories they need and/or want to tell. I watched students who clung to the corners slowly come closer and eventually tell a story. Students told fairytales and tales about wanting boyfriends. Students told stories they were currently writing and some that they read in books. Others told with an acoustic guitar and others simply told about what happened to them yesterday. The stories could range from 20 seconds to 17 minutes. Students told stories that were ready and some that were not. When requested, students also received feedback on the story that they decided to tell. What I learned is not to question what they told (unless it broke school rules) or why they came to the meetings.

I remember Charles (not his real name). Charles was the teenager my students avoided. He often threatened students and had an explosive temper. Rumor had it he carried a switchblade knife and was not afraid to use it. He came to the meeting but stayed at the edge of the group, listening as I told an original tale called "When did polar bears learn to dance?" It is a story about a little boy who could see dancing polar bears and a father who could not until he let down his guard and started to see what was not there, for his son's sake. When the group left, Charles asked me if he could tell that story. The next week he was not clinging to the wall but stood in front of everyone, and he shared the story better than I tell it. I never asked why he wanted to tell the story; I only knew he wanted to tell it. I did notice, however, that when his father picked him up, he never stopped yelling at Charles. I don't question what students tell but instead provide a place for them to tell their stories.

Creating the Agenda

I invited students to create the agenda. They decided on inviting tellers but having an open-mic format after the invited tellers. Students would sign up if they wanted to tell. The hours would be filled with stories.

Letting Go of the Agenda

Students come to a storytelling club for many reasons. Some arrived to share new stories, and others came simply because they might make a friend or had one at the meeting. Other times, they simply came to relax from the strain of school. After a hard practice, one of the students said to me, "Mr. Cordi, we are here for more than stories."

After that practice, I worked with my student board of officers and we changed the agenda. For the first 10 minutes of every meeting we simply used the time to catch up and informally greet one another. This became part of our tradition.

Later, we also played board games. I bought a quality karaoke machine and with my students sang to the eighties and a little Elvis. Letting go of the agenda helped us create a better sense of solidarity and, in truth, better storytelling practices because of the community we established. My students led me in a new direction with their ideas. Why not allow students to become leaders as well as tellers?

Empowering Students

Delegation was key to the success of Voices of Illusion.

One way to empower youth is to allow them to see and promote change. For example, my traditional training was to tell stories alone to an audience. However, my students were not raised to tell stories this way. They helped me change the way a story can be told. I have seen students tell with a partner, in small groups, and in groups of 30 for what I call "ensemble storytelling." Students tell in rap, with video, and with props. They revisit classic tales and place them in current times. One student physically tap-danced with a tale. Another shared a story using mime, and another student played heavy metal music between each story. They are empowered to do so.

The same type of empowerment can happen in a student storytelling group when a coach delegates the power in the group. One powerful way a student can grow is by sharing feedback on students' stories, but it must be done carefully.

Providing Feedback

Once students feel safe, invite them to share feedback with one another. I learned a technique from years of listening to student stories. Instead of having students say, "I liked this and I would fix this," have them offer observations and later on develop coaching from "inside of the story." As people hear and see the teller, in their minds they see the stories unfold. Students can retell what they saw, smelled, and experienced while the story was unfolding. They can tell from "inside the story."

Instead of suggestions, the students will say, "From your voice I could tell that Jack was afraid of the giant. I heard his voice quivering; I saw him shrink back when the giant picked up the boulder." "I could smell the fire the giant was building; it was the smell of a fresh fire burning pine." It is up to the students to use or not use what the others say they experienced, but often it leads the storyteller to deeper directions with the story. By working from "inside the story," the teller can see the way another person who is deeply listening sees the story. This can develop deeper listening skills and responding.

Students Can Set Future Directions

Student involvement leads to student investment. Students will come to you with many ideas. Students will want to build upon the great things you are doing together. They will want to form unity with the group. They will ask about creating membership cards or having T-shirts to identify the group. This is productive for the group. Decide what you or the group can afford, but don't be afraid to ask for financial help. The storytelling group is a good cause, and many groups, such as the Rotary and Optimist clubs, are happy to support your group. Students can also share good news of their work, and often they are skilled with social media and can help spread the word.

They will also want to tell more. To the same degree that you can delegate to the students, you can find other adult partners to help with the expansion of the group so the students have more opportunities for telling. If a nearby retirement residence requests students to come and tell, involve other adults and students in the planning, and celebrate their contributions and ideas. However, value your personal time. It is easy to allow yourself to be overburdened with storytelling needs; only do what you are comfortable doing. When you see this as a chore, it is time to reduce or revisit your work.

A special note: The students I worked with were teens, and some readers may think younger kids might not take on the same responsibilities. However, I have seen storytelling coaches for elementary and middle school whose students can voice when to take a break, where to find more stories, and help create design ideas for T-shirts or cards. While most younger kids don't get involved in planning where they tell, some do.

Stories brought my students and me together to create, collaborate, and build something greater. Supporting my students taught me to deeply listen, build together, and discover the joy, wonder, and educational value of sharing stories.

Still Listening to My Students

Years have passed since I coached Voices of Illusion, and I felt it was necessary to go back and ask the groups I worked with how they felt about their experiences. In the process, I can learn from them.

I remember Michelle Platenburg (then Austin), initially shy and even apprehensive. She first insisted that she was a story listener and was reluctant to tell. However, after some time, she said she had to tell. Her then-small voice became more and more powerful as she told. Not only that, I watched how she took on more and more leadership roles. She is now an elementary-school teacher. Here is what she shared about leadership:

> *I was co-chair for three plus years. I was very intimidated by this position at first because I was very shy as a high schooler and did not feel confident that I could be a leader. However, this experience helped me to gain confidence and leadership abilities that enabled me to excel in college as well as my career as a teacher. For future coaches/advisors of storytelling clubs I would highly recommend guiding the students to be student led. Students gain more experience when they are leading and organizing practices, meetings, and events. During my time, I remember Mr. Cordi often sitting back and observing/monitoring our meetings and events and only stepping in when we had questions, and always coaching us to be our very best.*

Heather Muela was not quite as shy as Michelle. Instead, she was curious and ambitious from the start. She joined not only the club but the traveling troupe. I watched how her writing ability grew, along with her ability to help others in both writing and telling. Every year I took the troupe to a professional recording studio, where we created a CD. She knew how important it was to revise, and she served to coach others in the process. Here she talks about her role as a coach of writing and telling. Heather is now a mother with two children, and I am sure she is coaching them as well. She said:

> *As peers in Voices of Illusion we would help one another in writing and editing each other's stories. Not only would I write and tell stories, I was also given the opportunity to lead. In leading we would be able to assist one another with writing, editing, and feedback in our performances. By receiving feedback, we*

were able to better ourselves … To critique someone else, you must first look into yourself to see the good and the bad that you bring. Recently I was a Den Leader for my son's Cub Scout group. From the start, I laid out my expectations. I made sure to let every boy know that they were special and they each played a huge role in our den. I learned this from my time in Voices.

Jessica Fritsch, a German exchange student, did not hold an official leadership position, but she came to see herself as a leader. She did not expect this to happen. Jessica recalled:

I never saw myself as a leader and [your] question made me think, a lot. Looking back at my times with Voices of Illusion, I indeed have been a leader. Maybe this was as a result of being a senior with mostly freshmen and some sophomores. I remember we did an urban legend show "Alligators in the Sewer" and in the show, we had to "prank" a teacher as we told the legend and the group elected me to do so because I carried so much of the show.

Lastly, as I think of the effects of a storytelling club or troupe, I turn to Kelly Rodriguez, who is now 32. It was with Voices that Kelly began to see the community that occurs when building a storytelling club. She shared with me that this is something you can't get in the school day. She shared:

In high school, storytelling was a wonderful connection not just to my peers but also a greater community in which I was welcomed. So much culture was shared in our small high school auditorium from seasoned storytellers, coming simply to invite us in to their world. I credit storytelling and drama in high school to a nearly unstoppable confidence, a willingness to embrace the silence and step forward when I'm not sure what the next step might be. To put myself out there, to be brave—storytelling gave me that. A deep appreciation for listening was also born out of storytelling. Quieting myself and deeply valuing the words of others has been invaluable in my adult life. As a Marriage and Family Therapist, it is literally my job to listen. To give the speaker space and for them to know I'm right there with them. To truly HEAR what the person across from me is saying and sit there with the words and feelings has been an incredible gift.

I work mainly with children and now, as a stay-at-home parent, my involvement in storytelling has been a huge asset. Just the other night, it was dark in the nursery, the boys were wanting one more story. And there was The Paperbag Princess, just sitting in my brain from a storytelling event when I was maybe 15. And there, snuggled in a twin bed, was a dramatic rendition, including voices and dramatic pauses. I can instantly join my children in play, in story,

in song, without hesitation. I can play, imagine, and create, which is something
adults often lose.

We choose fairy tales in my house, because I know that's what truly transports
children to magical places. We cherish the stories passed down, the stories of places
we will likely never travel. My children know the world to be a place of wonder,
because of the sense of wonder that was gifted to me when I was only 15.

Building Community

I remember it was finals week, and on that last day, most students wanted to go home and start summer vacation. However, my students stayed because we were invited to create a show and possible video on *Chicken Soup for the Teenage Soul* before it was released. (It would go on to become a *New York Times* best seller.) My students put in over 1,000 hours of practice making the show work. They didn't choose the stories, but they chose how they represented the stories. We made choices in our ensemble production. I directed, but so did my students.

We sent off the video, and upon receiving it, Jack Canfield, one of the creators of the *Chicken Soup for the Soul* series, cried at the power of the production. It is important to note: I didn't audition my students; I believe talent comes with time. My students competed with students from Paramount and Hollywood. However, their voices were selected. This does not happen in a school day. They were asked to share these stories.

Each week we did not prepare for an honor such as this but instead the honor of sharing stories together. We built community simply by listening and telling. It is two powerful practices that we don't do often in our daily lives. We honor our students when we listen to them. They honor one another when they are in this rich environment. When we let go of the idea that a storytelling club should be run by one person, we hold tight to the idea that we can make change and we can build a community, together. And that is a story worth telling!

CHAPTER 11

From Participant to Story Coach

BEN RUSSELL

Students come to C@W from many backgrounds, religiously and culturally speaking, but also in regard to experience in performance. They come from communities of varying diversity. Some students may never have met individuals from different religious traditions, while others may be minorities in their communities. Some may be nervous about what an interfaith storytelling group means. Some students have years of theatre experience, and others have never set foot on a stage. Every storytelling experience in C@W is different from the next, and we hope to make each one valuable to each teller.

I joined C@W when I was 14 years old. This was the first year of the program, and I had no idea what to expect. I had little experience in theatre, having played a minor character in one school play. I wasn't too sure what storytelling was. When I was younger, I loved the story *The Awongalema Tree*, told by actor Danny Kaye, and a few other tales I had on tapes. That's where my familiarity with storytelling ended.

Having been raised Jewish, I was used to being different from other people. I was familiar with Christianity and Hinduism, but I had no close friends of Islamic or other religious traditions. Having both a Jewish and a non-Jewish parent, I was well acquainted with both the value and the difficulty of interfaith relationships.

So it was that I, a shy 14-year-old, chose to participate in the first year of C@W. I went against my instincts, which constantly told me then (and often tell me now) not to get involved in things that I know nothing about. In an out-of-character moment, I joined the program. I never left. It was more than I could ever have expected, and more rewarding and life changing than I could ever have imagined.

It quickly became evident that I had nothing to be worried about in C@W. It didn't feel as if I was surrounded by people different from me, because at the heart of it we were all the same. We were all young people who were going through similar situations. Rapidly I found myself with many new friends from a wide variety of religious backgrounds. I learned that being from a different background doesn't make someone alien and unknowable. Instead, it ignites curiosity and gives us a score of new topics to discuss.

With a story of our choice, we were able to learn the process of storytelling. We went from the point of finding the perfect story to the point of being able to share the story with others. The atmosphere was always positive and allowed for experimentation, as the program focuses on giving appreciations rather than criticism. Sometimes a spur-of-the-moment addition to the story would be so well received that it would become a permanent component. Likewise, additions that elicited little response would organically be weeded out. The sessions helped me develop a worthy story, but equally important, they helped me develop self-confidence.

The program introduced me to and trained me in an art form that I fell in love with, one that can send powerful messages. Hearing cultural stories from the members of those cultures gives one a special insight into the "other." The stories were an outstretched hand welcoming us into something different. Gradually, what once seemed new and unfamiliar became relatable. Commonalities shone through the differences in the stories. Differences ceased to be scary and came to be valuable facets of interest.

Without even being fully aware of it, students learned about other peoples. Later on, as a college student, I studied different religions and found that I already had a point of reference. C@W had provided me with an insider's perspective. When I read the *Bhagavad Gita*, I already knew Arjuna and the Pandava brothers well. When I studied the rise of Islam, I already knew the events in the life of Muhammad. I had learned all that through enjoying stories, while others in my college classes were attempting to explore these matters for the first time.

I've returned to C@W as a story coach. Because C@W positively impacted me in so many different ways, I hope that with my help, it will do the same for others. It is so rewarding to see students' progress from nervous attempts at recitations of their stories to sharing them with smiles before members of the community. Sometimes a story touches on a subject unknown to the rest of the students, and afterward the group erupts in an eager discussion. Students grow positively in all respects in C@W. I am happy to have gone through the program and now help lead others to that same growth.

CHAPTER 12

Using C@W Approaches in the College Context

ADAH HETKO

I was one of the first youth storytellers with C@W, participating throughout high school. My C@W experiences inspired me to continue telling stories and doing interfaith work while I was studying at Oberlin College. After graduating, I began a two-year fellowship as Tanenbaum Inter-Religious Fellow at Vassar College. There I worked with student groups and other student-life offices on programming to support diversity and inter-religious growth.

In my work, I used my storytelling skills whenever I did any public speaking. When making decisions about programming, I often thought of the deep interfaith and intercultural experiences I'd had at C@W. I also explicitly taught storytelling in workshops and while preparing students for presentations.

Beyond interfaith peace building, I taught storytelling to address such topics as race, coming-of-age, science and religion, and women's empowerment. I approached these complex topics through teaching participants to create personal stories—stories from the tellers' own lives. Sharing personal stories helped participants articulate their identities, connect with larger issues, and build empathy across differences. Using personal stories also obviated questions of copyright and source. It left us free to use the content of the stories as we wished.

When designing programs, it was important to remind myself and others that storytelling is a tool for displaying content rather than a piece of content. Making this distinction often led to a conversation that clarified how storytelling could serve the purpose of a program. Rather than accepting a bullet point such as "Adah leads storytelling for 30 min." on a program outline, I worked with my co-leaders to develop prompts and framing appropriate to our goals.

In this chapter, I describe the structure of the programs I led, explain some approaches I found successful, and share a few of the exercises I used. I'm indebted to my C@W coaches, Mary Murphy and Marni Gillard, as well as my first storytelling teacher, Gert Johnson, for many of the ideas in this chapter. I'd also like to thank Reverend Sam Speers and Rabbi

Rena Blumenthal for their input and encouragement, Dr. Luis Inoa for his insight, and all of my participants for sharing their stories.

Storytelling as Team-Building Exercise

Storytelling can be a wonderful team-building exercise. I once led storytelling for a group of RAs who had been fighting. By the end of the exercise, they were giggling together and couldn't stop telling stories.

The format I used was the following storytelling round-robin. The following outline is for a 45-minute program on the theme of connection with nature, but the format can be adapted for any time slot or theme.

Storytelling Round-Robin

1. **Boot Camp and Example Story** (4 minutes)
   It's essential to welcome beginners into storytelling excitedly but also to ensure that the process is taken seriously. First, give a "30-second boot camp" and a short, engaging example story.

   In the 30-second storytelling boot camp, I say:
   - What is a story?
   - A story can be any scale, from "I got attacked by a wolf and almost fell off a cliff!" to "I was sitting under a tree and had this idea …" It can have lots of drama and action or share a very quiet epiphany.
   - A story has to have a beginning, a middle, and an end (an arc).

   Then transition into telling an example story based on the first prompt, such as "Tell the story of a joyful experience you've had while in nature."

   Prompt participants to practice appreciations by giving you appreciations on the example story. These should appreciate both the content ("Thanks for sharing such a meaningful story about your dad") and the way of telling ("I really liked how you imitated your dad's voice at the beginning. It made me feel like I got to know him").

2. **Prompts** (1 minute)
   Next, introduce the three story prompts that will be used in the round-robin. I like to use somewhat open-ended prompts that build on a theme. For the nature-themed round-robin, I use these:
   - Tell the story of a joyful experience you've had while in nature.
   - Tell the story of a challenging or sad experience you've had while in nature.
   - Tell the story of a moment when you felt deeply connected with nature.

3. **Storytelling Round-Robin** (30 minutes)
   First, ask participants to sit in two concentric circles, each facing a partner in the opposite circle. Explain that they will share stories with this partner, and then, when time is

called, one of the circles will rotate so that everyone has a new partner. When leading a round-robin in a room with fixed chairs or awkward seating, encourage participants to make sure they're facing their partner so they can easily make eye contact.

Next, set active-listening guidelines (no dialogue, listen fully). Explain that if partners have extra time at the end of their stories, they can just sit and smile at each other. It is important to discourage conversations, because dialogue distracts not only the speakers but everyone else in the room.

Round 1:   Joyful Experience (10 minutes total)
              Thinking (2 minutes)
              Person 1 tells (3 minutes)
              Appreciations (1 minute)
              Person 2 tells (3 minutes)
              Appreciations (1 minute)
Round 2:   Challenging or Sad Experience (10 minutes, same format)
Round 3:   Deep Connection (10 minutes, same format)

I time the activity strictly during the first round of stories. Then, as participants grow more talkative, I usually allow a bit more time for each round. It's very exciting to watch!

At the end, ask everyone to thank their partners.

4. **Debrief the Storytelling** (10 minutes)

Ask participants to regroup into one circle to debrief. Pose a question or two, such as:
- What was it like to share these stories?
- What was it like to listen to them?
- What worked? What didn't? What are some techniques you want to remember?
- What are some highlights from the stories that you heard?
- What will you take away from this experience?
- What did you learn about connecting with the natural world?

Finally, thank the group.

"Oh the Places I've Been"

"Oh the Places I've Been: Stories of Growing Older and (Maybe) Wiser," was started in 2012 by my predecessor, Joey Glick, who was inspired by a similar program at his alma mater, Colorado College. During each program, one campus mentor shares a life story for 20 minutes to an hour, followed by a Q&A or conversation. The event is held over lunch, and anyone on campus is invited to attend.

The programs varied tremendously. Some presenters chose to read excerpts of their writing, draw a timeline of their lives, lead a meditation, or share photographs, while others simply spoke. Many students asked for and received meaningful advice from beloved professors. Participants had moments of realization as well. I remember when one speaker and her listening colleague were both moved to tears after realizing that they shared similar hardships.

Faculty, staff members, and administrators who were known as mentors for students and colleagues were nominated as presenters, often by past participants. We invited our guests and scheduled events well in advance.

The week before the event, I met with the participant to review the structure of the event and prepare. If the participant needed prompting for his or her story, I would ask, "What brought you to where you are today?" or "What is one piece of your spiritual journey you would like to share?" or "What do you know now that you wish you had known when you were a college student?" If a participant had fully fleshed-out ideas, I would listen as he or she practiced the beginning of the story.

Understandably, participants were usually nervous at first. Thus, it was helpful to set a structure in which others would host and give a welcome, introduction, and closing. Often, attendees lingered long after the program to talk, which I took as a sign of success.

Interfaith Story Circle

We were lucky to have an adult Interfaith Story Circle (IFSC) near Vassar, led by storytellers Muriel Horowitz and Lorraine Hartin-Gelardi. I invited the IFSC to meet on campus several times, hosted by an interfaith student group. We followed the story circle's typical format. I guided the students in choosing a theme for each gathering, preparing an opening song or prayer, and a closing. I also helped the students prepare stories on the theme. These programs were always substantive intergenerational and interfaith exchanges.

Storytelling as Student Presentation

On several occasions, I prepared students to present stories for large audiences. One such program was a storytelling segment for "I Am Vassar," the Campus Life and Diversity Office's event during New Student Orientation. Select student leaders were invited to participate, and I coached the students in shaping personal stories about being at Vassar while having marginalized identities.

The "I Am Vassar" storytelling segment required extensive coaching. First, we met as a group for a two-hour session including round-robins and an overview of the program. In the next few days, the students sent me draft recordings of their stories. Then, I met with each student for individual coaching. Finally, we held another full-group coaching session and a run-through.

I worked to bring out the most polished stories possible and keep each story to between three and five minutes. I also had the responsibility of assuring the content was appropriate to our goals. Many of the stories centered around difficult struggles to find belonging at Vassar. How could I ensure the students' stories stayed within boundaries but allow them to be truthful? I encouraged the students to consider their audience of freshmen and to aim to inspire. I stressed that the stories weren't the totality of what they had to say but instead a performance of a sliver of their truth. I found success by coaching the students to focus on the points in the stories where they gained greater understanding or power.

With the stakes high for all of us, it was essential to build trust between me and the student tellers and among the student tellers. I involved the students in deciding the order of stories, where and how they sat, and whether or not applause would be invited.

Even after four sessions, I longed for more coaching time. But the students rose to the challenge. The audience of hundreds of students was fully engaged. They never checked their phones. Sometimes they whispered excitedly to one another or cheered. After the last story, the crowd sat for a moment in awe. Later, during orientation, I overheard many conversations sparked by the stories. Since the first year of implementation, the storytelling segment of "I Am Vassar" has been successfully repeated with new student storytellers.

If you are inspired to try a similar program at your college, here is an overview of our vision of the program, and a handout I gave the student storytellers.

"I Am Vassar" Storytelling Overview

Four or five students from a variety of backgrounds will share three-to-four-minute stories about an experience they've had at Vassar that gave them a fuller understanding of specific aspects of their identities, and how their identities are negotiated in the Vassar context. Here are two prompts that could help the participants find their stories:

Tell a story about a time you felt at home or did not feel at home at Vassar.
Tell the story of a moment of self-discovery during your time at Vassar.

In choosing stories, the presenters will be encouraged to select an experience that is very personal but not raw; something they have enough distance from to reflect on with maturity. In constructing the story, presenters will be asked to carefully consider the structure of their story and take into account the audience to whom they will be presenting. Participants will be required to return early to campus for a few practice sessions.

The process of selecting, constructing, and presenting the story will allow the tellers to better understand their lives at Vassar. In turn, for the freshman audience, the segment will provide specific grounding for discussions of identity, and model a constructive way to reflect on and share diverse experiences.

"I Am Vassar" Storytelling Handout

Structuring Your Story

What do you love about this story?
What are the essential elements (the bones) of the story? How can you emphasize them?

How can you make your transitions smooth?

What sensory details and body language can be added to enrich the telling?

Create a confident beginning and ending.

Take care of your audience: keep it simple and define terms they might be unfamiliar with.

Practicing on Your Own

If it helps you to write the story out, then write it out, but don't memorize word for word.

Tell it over and over to different people.

Draw a map or write out important details.

Tell the story to yourself in the mirror.

Record yourself telling your story and listen to the recording.

Time yourself and make sure you stay within the 3- to 4-minute range.

Performance Tips

Speak slowly and clearly, use eye contact, minimize nervous ticks, use body language intentionally. Dramatic pauses are great. Remember that everyone has their own style of telling.

Dress comfortably. Run through the scenes or emotional arc in your head right before telling.

Skill-Building Workshops

I led several workshops specifically intended to teach storytelling skills. One workshop for students began with a storytelling round-robin and progressed to other exercises. Many participants were excited to draw connections between the workshop and their classwork.

Another workshop, "Telling Our Stories," was presented as part of a student conference on sexual-violence prevention. First, three students that I had coached presented stories on their experiences overcoming interpersonal challenges. Then, I gave an overview of my storytelling theories. We ended with a Q&A, during which one participant after another raised her hand, offering a reason why appreciations, a skill I'd learned from C@W, were relevant to her work.

The final workshop I led was a train-the-trainer on storytelling for a small group of Vassar administrators. I knew already that storytelling had helped the students and faculty that I'd worked with reflect on their lives. I'd seen stories connect people. I'd even noticed how storytelling could shift power dynamics in a room, allowing the wisdom of an elderly person to be heard more clearly by a student or the insight of a student to be listened to more carefully by a professor. But it was during the train-the-trainer that one workshop participant clarified the essential effect of all those qualities: storytelling is social justice work! It can change the world! What more humane way to change it?

PART 2

C@W Coaching Exercises

MICKI GROPER, MARY MURPHY, NANCY MARIE PAYNE

CHAPTER 13

Body, Voice, and Breath

The exercises in this chapter help students to become more physically comfortable and breathe more efficiently while telling, and work on their vocal range.

13-1: Relaxing the Body in Segments

Step 1

- Stand with feet hip-width apart and weight evenly distributed.
- Focus on elbows and let them float gently up toward the ceiling.
- Repeat, focusing on wrists, then fingers.
- Stretch and imagine your fingers being pulled up toward the ceiling.

Step 2

- Let hands relax until they hang from wrists.
- Relax forearms so they hang loose from elbows.
- Relax arms so they drop down from shoulders.

Step 3

- Let the head drop forward, and continue so that the spine bends, vertebra by vertebra, from the top down, giving in to gravity.
- Let the knees relax so that the weight remains over the middle of the feet.
- Gradually build the spine back up again, vertebra by vertebra. Try not to tighten muscles. Allow the head to float up as a result of the neck vertebrae building one on top of the other.

Step 4

- Stand with eyes closed for a moment and be aware of your body.
- Then stretch, yawn, and shake out all over.

13-2: Stretching for Body Awareness

1. Stand with feet hip-width apart.
2. Lift arms toward the ceiling slowly, feeling as if you are being pulled upward by your fingers, as far as you can stretch.
3. Raise yourself onto your toes and hold for five seconds.
4. Let your feet flatten back to the floor and lower your arms slowly. Repeat.

13-3: Tightening Muscles to Relax

This exercise can be done sitting or standing. The leader should speak slowly.

Beginning with the toes, then moving to the feet, ankles, shins, and thighs, and continuing upward through the entire body:

1. Focus on the particular muscle group.
2. Tighten that muscle and hold a moment.
3. Relax. Repeat for the next muscle group.

13-4: Increasing Breath Control

Usually we breathe unconsciously. However, a storyteller needs to be able to take in more air than the average person and support his or her breath to use the air more efficiently.

1. Let the breath out completely. Wait until you feel the need for a breath. Breathe in. Repeat several times.
2. Draw in as much breath as you can. Feel your chest expand without raising the shoulders. Let air out slowly and steadily while producing an "s" sound.
3. Inhale deeply. Exhale, repeating the sound "heh" while pulling in stomach muscles with each exhalation of the sound. Repeat, using "ha" and "ho."

13-5: Awareness of the Body's Joints

1. Flex your joints, beginning with the toes and working upward through the body: ankles, knees, waist, fingers, elbows, shoulders, and neck.
2. Flex each joint rhythmically to a count of eight.
3. Repeat as desired.

13-6: Extending Vocal Range

This exercise is designed to gently stretch vocal limits without straining the voice.

1. Sit with arms extended out in front of you, palms facing the floor.
2. Sing "Hello" on each note of the arpeggio: do mi sol do.
3. Raise arms as the notes rise in pitch.
4. Repeat, raising the arpeggio upward by a whole step each time.
5. Continue with progressively higher notes until most reach their vocal limit.
6. Repeat from step one moving downward in pitch.

13-7: Increasing Volume and Strength of Voice

1. Hang arms, head, and torso downward, like a rag doll.
2. Bring arms and body up toward the ceiling, vocalizing a "whoop" sound.
3. Hold the pose briefly. Gradually drop arms, head, and torso, vocalizing "boom."

13-8: Expanding Vocal Flexibility

1. Repeat a sentence using different accents, tone qualities, and inflections. Use any familiar nursery rhyme or tongue twister the students know. Example: "It makes me laugh to see the calf go down the path to take a bath."
2. Repeat a sentence, expressing a different emphasis each time. Example: "What are you doing here?" or "I have to go now."

This exercise can also be done expressing different emotions.

Objectives

Coaches may wish to share the following objectives of the Body, Voice, and Breath exercises with students for self-reflection:

Students show physical comfort while performing.
Students use effective breathing techniques while telling.

Chapter 14

Icebreakers and Use of the Imagination

Exercises in this chapter help students become aware of the importance of speaking clearly, especially when using cultural terms and saying people's names. Students also explore their vocal ranges and learn how to use their hands and bodies to communicate ideas to audiences.

14-1: Saying Cultural Terms and Names Clearly

1. Leader provides copies of a sentence written without punctuation or spacing. Example: themoviestarmatthewsonisnowheretomeethisfans

2. Leader introduces the activity with this explanation: "Archaeology poses very unique problems. Explorers found an ancient text that had neither punctuation nor spacing. Knowledge of ancient vocabulary wasn't enough to interpret its meaning. Here is a problem similar to what they faced."

3. Participants scan the run-together sentence and must decipher it. (The name in the text could be Matt Hewson or Matthew Son. "Nowhere" could also be "now here.")

4. Leader explains: "Movie buffs might recognize the name 'Matt Hewson' or 'Matthew Son,' but without such background the name wouldn't be certain. The problem with 'now here' and 'nowhere' could go either way, but the meaning wouldn't be clear."

5. Leader continues: "Listeners, taking in your stories, get confused when you don't speak slowly and clearly. If someone shares a similar cultural background with you, he or she may have a better chance to understand references to your culture, even if you speak quickly. Those unfamiliar with culture-specific names and terms will get lost deciphering *what you said* and *what it means* to your tale. For example, when those unfamiliar with Sufi tales (ancient Muslim) hear 'Mullahnasruddin,' they hear the syllables but not a character's name. As listeners struggle to makes sense of any words or names, they miss a chunk of the story."

6. Leader demonstrates, saying his or her own name with a two-second delay between words. Example: "My name is Gertrude—one, two—Margaret—one, two—Alexander." Students say their names aloud, silently counting the two beats between the words.

7. Students are handed a printed list of everyone's names. In pairs they practice each other's name, speaking it slowly and clearly, and then introduce each other to the group.

Leader should stress that it is a matter of respect to pronounce your name in a way others can understand and a matter of respect to do the same when introducing someone else.

14-2: From Written Text to Oral Story

This exercise requires multiple copies of a very short folktale. See the Recommended Resources list in the appendix for books containing short tales.

1. Introduce the exercise by reminding students that spoken stories don't contain pictures for listeners (as in a picture book). However, when someone reading aloud or telling a tale imagines each scene and character, and uses imagery related to the senses, listeners enter the world of the tale and create pictures in their minds.
2. Divide the participants into groups. A coach or experienced storyteller should assist.
3. It helps if each group contains a diversity of ages, cultures, and storytelling experience.
4. One person reads the written form of the story aloud while the others read along silently.
5. A coach performs the story without the text in hand for all participants, modeling the skills of imagining each moment and character through gesture, dialogue, and using sense-related imagery (sounds, smells, textures, etc.).
6. Small-group members name what they could imagine—see, smell, hear—and how characters differed. They discuss the difference between the reading and the telling. Group leaders can encourage all to contribute what they noticed, helping newcomers take in the difference between reading and telling. The difference between a reader's and a teller's connection to listeners might also be noted.

Related activities include exercises 16-1 and 16-2.

14-3: Repeat After Me

This is one of several short exercises used to transition between the more consuming "working on stories" activities or rehearsals, which require a lot of focus.

1. A simple sentence such as "I live in the city" is spoken by the leader, and a few participants take turns repeating it differently with emphasis on a particular word.
2. Create a list of such sentences (or take suggestions) so each student can take a turn.

14-4: Speaking with Emotion

1. The leader says a sentence with little sense of emotion.
2. Pointing to each student in turn, the leader calls out an emotion and the student speaks the sentence with feeling and emotion-related movements. Example: "I am going to take care of my dog." Spoken with anger, affection, confusion, disgust, relief, etc. Students enjoy coming up with emotional tones and gestures.

14-5: Exploring the Use of Pauses in Performance

Moments of silence give listeners a chance to catch up to the teller. Pauses allow the teller to relax. Tellers can share how a pause affected the audience or the teller's awareness of performance skill. This exercise, especially helpful for beginners, is from *Creative Communication* by Fran Averett Tanner.[1]

1. Distribute a relatively lengthy written statement or description, such as "I was alone late at night in the house. I heard something pound at the window. Cautiously I approached and there, staring at me, was a horse!"
2. Someone reads it aloud with no pauses.
3. Take turns pausing to affect emphasis and create meaning. Notice how various readers find alternative rhythms and places to put emphasis, simply through pausing. Encourage students to offer short sections from the stories they are working on.

14-6: Show Yourself

1. Students stand in a circle.
2. Each in turn says his or her name with style and strikes a pose or uses a gesture that reflects something about who he or she is.
3. All other students chorally speak the person's name and copy the motion, reflecting the style they observed.

14-7: The Magic Ball

1. Students stand in a circle.
2. One student creates an imaginary ball and proceeds to pull and shape the ball into the form of some useful object.
3. The student then pantomimes using the object.
4. The other students guess what the object is.
5. The object is then "rolled" back into an imaginary ball and is tossed to another student, who continues the game.

14-8: Don't Make Me Laugh!

This is an excellent icebreaker for elementary and middle school students. It provides a fun way to learn how to focus and use eye contact as an effective tool. It's especially useful when the students don't know each other.

During the exercise, the coach reads the following "action poem" (or sings it to the tune of "Ballin' the Jack"):

First you look your partner in the eyes.
He will want to laugh—that's no surprise.
You can raise your eyebrows nice and high.
Then you twist your mouth, and twist your nose,
Funny faces will fly.
Make your partner laugh, He's out—you win!
Get a new partner, then begin . . .

1. Students stand in parallel lines, each facing a partner.
2. They make eye contact with the goal of remaining straight-faced.
3. A coach recites the "action poem" and asks one row at a time to make faces in an attempt to make the partner opposite laugh.
4. If a participant laughs, that person sits down. The teller who's left finds another partner among those still standing.
5. Play continues until the poem has been offered a few times. All those left standing are declared winners.

14-9: Pass the Clap

In this exercise, participants play a game that teaches them to use eye contact and develop quick reflexes.

1. Participants stand in a circle.
2. One person starts by turning to the person on his or her right. Facing each other, both make eye contact and clap their hands simultaneously.
3. The second person (to the right of the one who started) now turns to the person on his or her right. They make eye contact and clap simultaneously.
4. The "clap with eye contact" continues around the circle.
5. Once everyone has gotten to clap, the game can continue with claps moving in both directions. It gets a little crazy, but it's a fun icebreaker and helps students look at each other.

14-10: Show What You Say

The leader gives each student a sentence to say. The student gets the gist of the sentence, sets down the paper, and speaks it while performing an action that "shows" the words. Example sentences:

- Mary looked to the top of the mountain.
- The general walked into the room.
- The tiger roared.
- Peter had never seen the ocean before.

14-11: Miming

This call-and-response activity can be done in a large circle or in small groups with one leader per group. Most of our call-and-response activities came about and evolved from a need to demonstrate a particular technique for the students and involve them in a fun way.

1. The leader has a list of actions and calls one to each student. Example: "Holding a helium balloon that is trying to carry you away."
2. The students express the actions through their movements only. The leader is the only one speaking during this exercise. Students can contribute scenes or specific movements they've found in the stories they are telling. They enjoy and learn from watching one another's movements.

14-12: Sculpting Each Other

1. Students pair up. In each pair, one person is the sculptor and the other one is the clay.
2. The leader whispers a directive to the sculptor, who, in turn, fashions the "clay," positioning his or her partner accordingly. Examples: Create a sculpture of a hero, a person who is afraid, a small child building a sandcastle, someone riding a horse, a king or queen, or a moment of joy (or any other emotion).
3. The sculptor steps back to show the "work" is complete, and one at a time the group guesses what the sculpture represents.
4. The activity is repeated so each person has a chance to be both sculptor and clay.

Objectives

Coaches may wish to share the following objectives of the Icebreakers and Use of the Imagination exercises with students for self-reflection:

Students are aware of the importance of clear enunciation.
Students take into account cultural differences.
Students have experimented with their vocal ranges—i.e., volume, pace, tone, emotion.
Students can convey and communicate ideas through use of their hands and bodies.

Endnote

1. Fran Averett Tanner. 1969. *Creative Communication*. Clark Publishing Company.

CHAPTER 15

Choosing a Story

These exercises encourage students to choose stories that speak to their own faiths and cultural traditions, engage them deeply, and are suitable for telling to audiences of all ages and backgrounds.

15-1: Choosing Stories for Diverse and Interfaith Audiences

The following is a list of instructions for coaches to share with students as they choose stories for telling to diverse and interfaith audiences. It comes from a C@W handout found in the appendix. When doing this exercise, first present the students with the C@W Guidelines for Choosing Stories (see appendix).

- Choose a story that you love. Pick it because it moves you, and you believe it will affect others. Whether it is serious or funny, know why you like the story and feel it is right for you.
- The story should say something special about your culture, religion, or traditions or beliefs you cherish; and you should want others to know about these aspects of your world.
- Remember that while storytelling is about sharing aspects of your faith and culture, it's never about converting others to your beliefs.
- Be sure that if your story includes religious terms, references to holidays, historical events, or practices, you give your listeners enough information either at the beginning of the story or when you use the term.
- A "wisdom tale" or story that imparts a general truth or piece of wisdom can be a good choice. Several such tales are shared by many cultures. Try to bring a flavor of *your* culture to the way you tell it.
- In an introduction before your telling, it's fine to acknowledge that stories from many traditions may illustrate the same truth or impart the same wisdom.
- Always remember that others' beliefs or practices may be very different from yours. Great richness and insights often come because of the diversity.
- Be aware that the story you choose for an interfaith audience may be different from one you'd tell to listeners from your own tradition.

- Consider whether there is anything about the story that might be offensive to another group of people or cause them harm. You want to be especially careful to avoid presenting hurtful stereotypes or portraying people of a particular tradition in an unfavorable way. Tell your story to rehearsal partners and/or your group's leader with this in mind. If this seems to be a possibility, your best choice is to look for a different story to share.

15-2: Sharing Literature from One's Tradition

1. Students are encouraged to bring a number of printed stories, picture books, or collections of tales from their faith traditions so the group can explore the wealth of available material. The aim is for both new and experienced tellers to be aware of all the places stories exist.
2. Participants are asked to choose one item from the display table, explore it, and then either share their exploration experience, summarize a story they encountered, or talk about the importance of that collection or holy book to their tradition.
3. In turn, students respond to one (or a few) speakers, or name something they learned from listening to the group sharing.
4. Coaches ask who knows, or is considering, what story he or she will work on over the next weeks as they move toward a performance. Or they might inquire about something each student learned about another culture from the exploration activity.

EXTENSION: Sometimes the group is introduced to performance telling by one or more experienced student tellers. Those who perform share what drew them to that particular tale and something of the process of finding and working on the piece.

Objectives

Coaches may wish to share the following objectives of the Choosing a Story exercises with students for self-reflection:

Students have chosen or created stories to tell that connect to their faiths or cultural traditions in ways that they are able to articulate.
Students have chosen stories that are appropriate for other students and for family audiences of all backgrounds.
Students have chosen stories that closely follow the Guidelines for Choosing Stories (see appendix).
Students have chosen stories that they like and that move them.

CHAPTER 16

Advancing the Development of a Story

Using the exercises in this chapter, coaches assist students to tap into their imaginations to develop the characters, settings, and plots of their stories.

16-1: Fleshing Out the Characters

1. Divide the participants into groups diverse in age, culture, and experience in storytelling. Each group needs a coach or experienced group leader.

2. For about two minutes, each participant describes one character from his or her story. A few listeners reflect details they learned from the teller's description.

3. The leader explains that it is easier to describe someone we *know* than a character we've only encountered through the written word. The leader now asks questions to help each teller more fully imagine the character he or she described. In order to "step inside the story" and imagine their characters, students might find it helpful to close their eyes or simply look off into the distance as they hear the questions. They can make up answers to any questions not provided by the story. What they make up should "fit" with the tale.
    * Name your character or create a name. How tall is he or she?
    * What color is his or her hair, skin, eyes, teeth?
    * See the character's clothing and shoes: color, cleanliness, size, plain or frilly, new or old?
    * Does the character care about, or take care of, his or her appearance?
    * Does the character have a pet or like animals? Which animals?
    * What is the character's favorite food, color, and season? Why?

4. Each member of the group now re-describes his or her character to the group.

5. The leader asks what new details might be added to the story or how the questions brought the student a better understanding of the character. If a "made up" trait isn't important to the story plot, it can still be useful in making the character seem real. The leader encourages further work on other characters. Once all tellers are working steadily on their performances, they try the exercise once again.

EXTENSION: Each teller stands as if the character is facing someone in authority, walking in a crowd, caught in a rain storm, missed lunch. Each teller stands as if the character is primarily mean, kind, scared, hopeful, nervous, confident, or some other trait.

16-2: Being in Your Setting

By knowing your story's setting intimately, you tell a more believable story, one the audience pictures. Some of what tellers imagine may be put into the telling but not every detail. Simply by imagining the setting in more detail, the teller enables the audience to experience it.

Step 1

The coach leads the group slowly through a guided visualization, asking key questions to encourage tellers to make up and imagine the details of the settings of their stories:

1. As a character, look around the place where your story begins (or moves to).
2. Look down at the surface you are standing on. What is it?
3. Look straight ahead. What do you see?
4. Look to the left, right, behind yourself. What is there?
5. What is the season? Temperature? Light source?
6. Take a deep breath. What do you smell?
7. Reach out and pick up something that is close by. What is its weight? Color? Size? Shape? What is it? What use does the thing have in the story?
8. Listen for sounds. Make a sound that is part of the story's setting.

Step 2

The leader in each group walks the group, as listeners, through a character's setting.

Step 3

Each participant finds a partner to guide through his or her setting from the point of view of a character. Tellers can walk around the setting pointing out objects or even hand things to their listeners, making the telling interactive. They might describe aromas or make sounds.

Step 4

The leader reassembles the group and asks each person to share one thing he or she experienced in his or her setting. A few individuals might take the whole group through their settings if time allows. Students might be asked to describe how something they imagined would work in the story or, even if it wasn't important to the plot, how it could help make the setting real for listeners.

16-3: Story Pyramid

Students seem to learn their stories more easily and gain new insights after doing this exercise from Karen Chace's book, *Story by Story*.[1]

1.   Students create this pyramid to see their stories from another angle:

_____

Name of main character

_____

Two words describing main character

_____

Three words describing the setting

_____

Four words stating the problem

_____

Five words describing one event

_____

Six words describing the second event

_____

Seven words describing the third event

_____

Eight words describing the solution

2.   Students share their work out loud with a small group or the entire group. Everyone listens.

16-4: Character Creation

Students draw a stick figure with a full face and write descriptions on it, following these prompts:

1.   Represent your character's emotional state at an important point in the story.
2.   On one arm, write a word (or words) that best describes that emotion.
3.   On the other arm, choose a few words that describe the character's body.
4.   On one leg, write a few words that describe how the character would walk.

5. On the other leg, describe how the voice of the character would sound when he or she speaks.

6. On the vertical line down the middle of the body, describe a gesture the character might use.

16-5: Story Bones

Students write out the answers to these prompts and share their answers orally:

1. Who is your main character?
2. Who are key supporting characters?
3. Where does your story take place? Does the story end in a new place?
4. Describe the main story setting using at least three descriptive words.
5. What is the main problem in the story?
6. Describe two things you can see.
7. Describe one emotion or trait that a character's speech reveals.
8. Describe two gestures important to your story.
9. How does your story end?
10. What do you love most about this story, or why did you choose *this* story?

Objectives

Coaches may wish to share the following objectives of the Advancing the Development of a Story exercises with students for self-reflection:

Students have brought their stories to life by knowing the characters, sharing details, and making them real by using their imaginations.
Students have visualized and created fully developed characters.
Students have visualized and created fully developed settings.
Students have visualized and created fully developed plots.

Endnote

1. Karen Chace. 2014. *Story by Story.* Marion, MI: Parkhurst Brothers Inc.

CHAPTER 17

Creating Stories from Our Own Imaginations

Students develop the tools to quickly dream up new stories and effectively retell existing stories in these exercises.

17-1: How and Why Tales

Students love this exercise. In a few simple steps, students who have been working on their own stories take a break and quickly compose, learn, and tell a story with a beginning, middle, and end. It's all the other exercises rolled into one. Afterward, students seem to feel proud of their ability to write and tell their own stories.

1. Students do the creative work of coming up with a question. Examples: Why is the sky blue? Why do turtles move slowly?
2. Each student answers his or her chosen question by blocking out a simple plot with a beginning, middle, and end.
3. They tell their stories to the class using all the storyteller's tools they've being exploring, showing characters and setting through gesture and voice.

17-2: Magic Key

Keys of assorted shapes and sizes are needed for this exercise. Put the keys in a container or spread them out on a table.

1. Each student picks a key.
2. Students are asked to create an original short story about their key. With the help of the following questions, they are to block out a beginning, middle, and end. Students are offered the questions aloud one at a time, slowly, while they make notes on paper:
    *   Where did you find the key?
    *   What does the key unlock?

- What did you find once the lock was opened?
- What did you do about it?

3. Students tell their stories until each has had a turn.

Students enjoy creating stories at a moment's notice for this exercise. They can also work together to tell in tandem.

17-3: Story Retelling

1. The coach asks students to picture the setting, characters, and action of a story they are about to hear.
2. The coach asks students to form groups of three or four before the telling begins and instructs them that they will retell the tale as a group, each member telling part of the story before another member of the group takes over. They are asked to choose the order in which they will retell the tale.
3. The coach tells a simple folktale with plenty of expression, modeling the qualities and techniques of storytelling the students have already been learning.
4. One student begins the retelling until the coach rings a bell or claps his or her hands to signal that the next student in the group is to continue. The retelling proceeds and can begin again if all the groups aren't finished.
5. Finally, one teller from each group is chosen to tell solo.

EXTENSION 1: Each group turns the story into a play. After a brief rehearsal, each group performs its unique creation for the reassembled large group. They are encouraged to be "innovative" as they make a drama. Appreciations are offered for creative choices. Students might also share how the exercise gave them insights into improving the stories they are working on for performance.

EXTENSION 2: Instead of a coach telling the story, each group of students sketches out a character, setting, and plot for an original tale. Silly or incongruous ideas are acceptable. In just seven minutes, the group tells the story one by one, as before, or acts it out as a play.

EXTENSION 3: Students are paired to retell each other's original stories or the story they've heard their partner rehearse for performance. If they volunteer to tell another's story to the larger group, they must ask permission of the original teller. *(This third extension just happened one day when one of the younger students said he wanted to tell the story he had been hearing from a much-respected older student. That teller gave permission, and the younger child retold the tale to everyone's delight. The older teller said he got some good insights watching and listening to himself being imitated. We've have fun with this activity ever since. Only once did a student not want his tale told by another. – NMP)*

Objectives

Coaches may wish to share the following objectives of the Creating Stories From Our Own Imaginations exercises with students for self-reflection:

Students can plan new stories using all the tools of a storyteller.
Students can retell stories in an impromptu fashion using all the tools of a storyteller.

CHAPTER 18

Practicing Storytelling Techniques

This chapter offers exercises that help students learn how to use microphones; add emotion and drama to their performances with their voices, postures, and expressions; and choose impactful openings and endings for their stories.

18-1: Microphone Use

Students need practice using microphones. It enables them to gain confidence in using the equipment and to more closely experience the sound of an actual performance.

It's good for them to try a variety of microphones, such as handheld mics, those that rest in a stand, and those that have a long lead, allowing the teller to travel around the stage. Working with headsets and clip-on microphones is helpful, too.

Students should learn about the correct distance between the mouth and each particular type of microphone, listening for volume and tone, "popping" consonants, etc. They should also learn to use mics in such a way that their mouths can be clearly seen by their audience as they speak, which may mean learning to hold the mic a bit under their mouths.

Students should take the time to tell at least part of their story on each kind of mic.

18-2: Say It How?

The intention or thought behind words influences how they are spoken and how they are understood by their audience.

1. Give each student a word to say from a list. Examples: when, where, now, dry, you, enter, stop, please.
2. Assign a feeling with which the word should be said. This works best if the word and feeling don't go naturally together. For example: "Say 'please' as if you are bored to tears."
3. Have the student say the word with several different feelings: regret, fear, pride, anger, surprise, sarcasm, pleading, etc.
4. Have the class notice and point out body tenseness, posture, gestures, facial expressions, and so on as the same word is said with different feelings.

18-3: Storyboarding or Story Mapping

Before you begin, hand out one sheet of newsprint and a marker, pencil, or crayon to each student.

Step 1

Each student creates a storyboard or story map.

Storyboard: The coach explains storyboarding, a technique used by filmmakers to lay out the plot of a story in a simple visual form. It helps the creator see the progression of a tale and notice any gaps in the story line. To create a storyboard:

- Students are asked to draw "cartoon blocks" on the page, starting with eight but leaving room for more to be added if needed.
- They are to tell the story by drawing pictures, moving from block to block.
- They are encouraged to use simple stick figures. Some students who to love to draw will get bogged down in the art, rather than in the blocking out of the story.
- They move to a new square when the scene changes or a new character enters.

OR

Story Map: A story map might be used to show the layout of a story scene or even to show movement from scene to scene. In creating a story map:

- Key buildings or other structures, roads, mountains, rivers, and other elements of a landscape might be important to map.
- The characters might be simply sketched or appear as symbols or even letters.
- The story is told by moving from map feature to map feature.
- Sometimes key words that are repeated in a story or moments of action might appear on a map.

Step 2

Students form groups of three or four participants and take turns telling their stories using their storyboards or story maps.

EXTENSION: On occasion, the large group gathers to see how others have used these formats to work on their stories. A few students may tell their stories to the whole group.

18-4: Openings and Closings

1. Coaches demonstrate various ways to take the stage and begin a performance. Often an introduction is appropriate so the audience gets attuned to the teller's voice. Examples: "My name is …" "The title of my story is …" "This tale relates to today …"

2. A coach or experienced teller models how to use space and movement when entering the performance space. The introduction might be followed by a pause, lowering of the head, taking a step backwards, or an appropriate segue from introduction to story.

3. A participant steps into the circle of tellers (or onto a stage) to experiment with a performance opening. Key points:
   - Tellers do well to connect to the audience verbally or non-verbally before beginning the tale.
   - Some tellers prefer not to introduce the story. Yet "taking the stage" and silently connecting to the audience before a strong story opening is recommended.
   - Stories can begin with "Once upon a time" or other traditional openings such as "Crick crack" or "Ho" from particular cultures. Traditions are part of storytelling but should be researched, especially in an intercultural community.
   - Sometimes a dramatic gesture, change of tone, or different stance signals the story's start.

4. Each participant proceeds as above, practicing the opening of his or her story. The exercise can be repeated a second time or another day to experiment with or to practice openings.

5. Coaches show ways to bring a story to a close. Key points:
   - Slowing down the pace or softening the voice are ways to alert the audience the story is ending.
   - Saying "The end" is not a particularly artistic choice, but young tellers like it.
   - Certain traditional cultural phrases fit as story endings.
   - Lowering of the head, bowing, and stepping back are gestures that signal the end.
   - Above all, a teller should wait briefly for the audience to take in the final image of the tale and experience that the telling is over.
   - Often, the audience expresses its appreciation through applause, and a teller should never exit too quickly, nor stay too long.
   - The closing of a performance might include: "Thank you for listening," "It has been my pleasure," etc.
   - The more a teller is aware and plans, the better the show goes.

18-5: Over the Top

1. A coach explains that overacting can hurt a performance, yet sometimes exaggeration works effectively. "Over the top" just might mean it's *too* much.
2. A coach calls out a sentence, with no exaggeration, and chooses a student to add gestures, tones, and word-rhythms that might be great exaggerations.
3. The group copies what the student has done.
4. Another student tries an exaggeration that would be considered "over the top."

5. Students say lines from their own stories, with both appropriate and "over the top" exaggerations.

EXTENSION: This activity can be used to help students add humor to their stories.

Objectives

Coaches may wish to share the following objectives of the Practicing Storytelling Techniques exercises with students for self-reflection:

Students use a wide vocal range in their stories and practice with microphones.
Students have different ways to add expression, emotion, and drama to their stories.
Students change their voice, posture, and expression to give emphasis to their stories.
Students have chosen openings and closings for their stories.

Excerpts from Formal Letters of Support

To Whom It May Concern:

> One of the main goals of our school is to instill in our children a sense of pride in themselves and to inspire a sense of responsibility towards the community in which they live. Approximately two years ago, our school was blessed with an opportunity that we never expected. We were approached by Gert Johnson and Paula Weiss to participate in a wonderful program called Children at the Well.
>
> One cannot imagine the benefit we received as a school and as a community. It opened a door of understanding for our students and our teachers. Our students had opportunities to build friendships with children of other faiths, visit other places of worship, and share their own stories and faith. Throughout the years, we have participated in interfaith programs that were adult oriented. This program was the first that reached out to the youth, our future generation. If we affect the hearts of our youth, this will affect community change for generations to come....
>
> — Sharifa Din; Principal:AnNur Islamic School, Albany NY

> ...Both Ms Johnson and Ms Weiss have committed themselves to the fundamental principle that when we gather children together and encourage them to be who they are, they will learn acceptance and tolerance and (this is no surprise to educators) they learn more about themselves. As a Protestant minister I have been blessed to be part of this program to share how my faith tradition uses stories and have been amazed to be in a room of youth from a wide variety of faith backgrounds who genuinely like each other. In a world that increasingly divides itself along sectarian lines I find Children at the Well to be a strong source of hope.
>
> — Rev. Kent Busman; Director: Camp Fowler, Speculator, NY

> ...I strongly urge that Children at the Well be supported so that it can continue to do the great work of gathering the many different interfaith and culturally varied members of the capital district. No other path or method has done it so well. There is urgency in today's world for a deeper understanding of each other, to not remain foreigners and recognize that there is unity in diversity. Children at the Well provides that possibility of invitation, of gathering and recognition and honoring of differences and the desire for connection amongst all. What a garden the world would be if story telling by children from different faith groups became a way of understanding each other
>
> — Jyoti Swaminathan, Psy.D. Teacher, HinduTemple, Capital District, NY.

Photo credit: Robert Cooper

All photo credits this page: Robert Cooper

Written Comments by Audience Members, after Performances:

Dear Storytellers,

Thank you for coming to St. Paul the ApostleParishCenter on Sunday, March 18th. I enjoyed hearing every story. You all did a wonderful job. Your stories have been sticking in my head all day yesterday and today. You all get a "10" for presentation and performance!"

— Signed, A member of the audience

"I am in awe of the wisdom and grace these young storytellers are so capably sharing with us all. Thank you."

"I am really proud of my son being part of this great group where every culture and religion is just one story or part of one great story and that is the story of our world- all inclusive. We are one."

"Fabulous experience! I am so pleased to see how your organization encourages and enables young people to speak publically. It is a wonderful way to gain and affirm confidence and positive self-image as well as developing skills in language and creativity."

— Joan Goodman, PhD.

"I want you to know that we appreciate everything that C@W has done. The children have definitely transformed into more confident public speakers!"

"Great presentations! Must have been great mentoring.""I was so glad I came. I really enjoyed the stories""It was absolutely lovely and inspiring"

"Everybody spoke very well, and the tellers were very comical. It was a great laugh!"

"I love to be part of something so positive and something that promotes people of different cultures and faiths sharing. The young adults who present and share their stories inspire me to be a better person. I leave here with a warm heart and a smile on my face ☺"

"C@W has been such an important factor to carve our children's personality and future. The coaches are doing a tremendous job in helping our kids be comfortable with themselves for who they are and their faith..."

"Though varied in their abilities, the children demonstrated a wonderful unity in their collective mission, to celebrate our similarities and respect our differences."

"It's very impressive to see the maturity and confidence in these young people. I admire their ability to speak in public and tell their stories in an animated fashion, delighting the audience."

"To bring children together with one vision- to carry joy through story- what a great gift for this community- may it spread!"

Written Comments from Participants, at the End of the Season:

"...Before this project, I had learned about other faiths, but had never met anyone with a different faith than my own. I enjoyed this project because it opened me up to all kinds of new people and friends with different faith traditions like the Muslim, Hindu and Jewish..."

"...One thing that really surprised me was the way I changed once I wanted to change myself and my quality of telling once I committed myself. This project was very beneficial to me and I hope I helped myself and others to bring understanding and peace to the world, whether we believe in Islam, Christianity, Judaism, Confucianism, Buddhism..."

"I enjoyed being part of Children at the well because it motivated me to become a better person. I learned lessons from religions other than my own...I enjoyed learning from my fellow peers as they told their stories and discussed certain aspects of their religion with the group...Thank you so much for your patience, lessons, and wisdom."

"The last 6 years of C@W have made me infinitely happy. I love you all!"

Photo credit: Mars Fotographi

Appendix

You can download the forms, letters, and lists in this appendix at childrenatthewell.org and adapt them to suit the needs of your storytelling group.

Sample Student Nomination Slip

STUDENT NOMINATION SLIP

FOR POTENTIAL PARTICIPANTS IN THE CHILDREN AT THE WELL PROJECT

To assemble our group of young people, we ask for assistance from teachers or others in nominating students whom they feel have potential as storytellers and have sufficient maturity to commit to our project. Ideal candidates are willing to meet others and engage in something new. Students should be from grades six to nine. Please see the accompanying brochure for information about us, and call or write if you have any questions.

Please let the students' parents know that you are making this nomination, and secure their verbal consent to give us contact information for the students.

Thanks very much for your help!

Name of teacher nominating student : _____

School : _____

Name of student being nominated : _____

Age and grade level of student : _____

Have the parents given consent to have contact information made available to us? _____

If so, please enter contact information for student.

Email address: _____

Mailing Address: _____

_____

_____

Phone number: _____

Please briefly describe the qualities you see in this student which led you to make this nomination. (Use back of sheet as well, if necessary.)

Please return forms to:

Sample Application Letter

Dear

Thanks for your interest in applying to join Children at the Well. We started this youth storytelling program in 2006 so that kids of many faiths and backgrounds could learn storytelling together. So far as we know, we are the only storytelling group of this kind!
Here is some information about our upcoming C@W season:

- A group of students from different traditions will meet with professional story coaches each Sunday afternoon from January 4th to April 26th, 2015, on Sunday afternoons from 2 to 4:30 to learn about storytelling, choose stories to tell that they feel connect to their own traditions, and work on their stories to prepare for a public performance on April 26th. It would be important to come to all, or most, of our meetings.
- We'll be meeting at First Unitarian Universalist Society of Albany, 405 Washington Ave., Albany NY 12206.

You can find more information about C@W at childrenatthewell.org or by contacting me.

Now, we'd like to know more about you. Please write a note back to tell us a bit about yourself and explain why you would like to be involved. The questions below can help you get started in writing. Don't feel you have to answer every question.

- Have you done any storytelling in the past?
- Is there anyone in your family who is a good storyteller? If so, what do you like about their stories?
- Do you have a story about your own tradition or from your family or your own life that you find yourself telling to other people?
- Is there a story that you particularly like to hear?
- Storytelling involves practicing. Would you be willing to put the time in to practice storytelling?
- This project will involve sharing with people of other traditions. Would you be interested in that?

You can send your note by email to me at directorcaw@gmail.com. Thanks again for your interest. I'm looking forward to reading what you send, and sharing it with our staff!

Sincerely,

Paula B. Weiss
Director, Children at the Well

Sample Permission Form

NAME OF STUDENT _____

DATE OF BIRTH OF STUDENT _____

PHONE NUMBER(S) _____

HOME ADDRESS _____

EMAIL ADDRESSES _____

EMERGENCY CONTACT and PHONE (SHOULD PARENT NOT BE AVAILABLE): _____

I, (please sign name), _____, give my permission to have my son/daughter participate in the Children at the Well coaching sessions, held at Christ Our Light Catholic Church. I also give my permission for my son/daughter to take part in storytelling rehearsals and performances at various locations (with advance notice) throughout 2017, and to be driven there if need be, by staff of Children at the Well, or by another parent.

PICTURE/INFORMATION RELEASE

I hereby authorize _____ to participate in public awareness efforts in the framework of WithOurVoice Inc.'s programs. These efforts may consist of advertisements, publications, and presentations. I give my permission for any photographs or video of my son/daughter to be used in these efforts.

Also, I give my permission for my son/daughter to participate in a process to help look at the overall effectiveness of our programs.

Your child is in no way obligated to participate in any of these efforts. This is the choice of the parent/guardian and the child. Any assistance in this matter will be greatly appreciated.

Signature of Participant: _____

Date: _____

Signature of Parent/Guardian: _____

Date: _____

I have had sufficient opportunity to read this document. I have read and understood it, and I agree to its terms.

Signature of Participant: _____

Print Name: _____

Signature of Parent/Guardian: _____

Date: _____

Sample Info Alert

<u>Welcome to our 2015 Children at the Well Tellers!</u>
This will be a great year…our tenth!!…with lots of exciting things planned

Our first meeting will be Sunday, January 4th, 2 to 4:30 p.m., at 405 Washington Ave., Albany

We'll be at the home of the First Unitarian-Universalist Society of Albany. Parking is on the street (Western Ave. or West St. usually have plenty of spots) or across Washington Avenue in the SUNYA parking lot at the corner of Washington Avenue and the section of Robin St. that runs between Washington and Western Aves.

We'll meet each Sunday after that (but not Easter) to April 26th. Please mark your calendars!

ALL PARENTS MEETING: *Sunday, January 11th, 2:00–3:00 p.m. at FUUSA.*

Please note- on January 25th, we'll meet at Eastern Parkway United Methodist Church, 943 Palmer Ave., Schenectady 12309, to attend the **Winter Lights** storytelling and music performance- **please plan to attend, everyone- and invite friends and family!**

There will be off-site rehearsals April 19th (some may be in the morning) and we'll have a Sunday April 26th performance and potluck supper at FUUSA, and an evening Youth Circle during the week.

Some reminders**: Please be on time! We will begin promptly each week at 2:00 p.m.** If you must be late, if you will miss a session, or have weather related concerns, please contact Paula ahead of time.

Permission Slips: If you can, please print it, fill out, sign, and return. I'll have forms available on Sunday, too.

Staff:

Paula Weiss	Director, XXXXX@gmail.com
Nancy Marie Payne	Coach, XXXXX@juno.com
Micki Groper	Coach XXXXXX@aol.com
Ben Russell	Coach, XXXXXX@gmail.com
Danielle Charlestin	Assistant Coach, XXXXX@gmail.com
Allison Lerman-Gluck	Assistant Coach, XXXXXXX@gmail.com

<u>Schedule of visitors to C@W</u>—*parents, you're welcome to join us for the presentations at 3:30, on these days:*

Feb 1—Beth Sabo Novik
Feb. 8—Jacqui Williams
Feb. 22—Jyoti Swaminathan
March 8—Marni Gillard

Sample Contacts Form

This "Kid Grid" chart is one of the first things we put together each year once we've gathered a group of students for an upcoming season. It is extremely useful for parents, students, and coaches. Before finalizing it and handing it out, we always check with parents first to be sure they are comfortable sharing contact info with others, and to be sure we have the best possible contact info for each family.

NAME	PARENT(S)	PHONE(S)	EMAIL ADDRESS(ES)	MAILING ADDRESS
Abhinav Mehta				
Atharv Agashe				
Ayah Osman				
Farriya Thalho				
Kalyan Ramkumar				
Peter Meshkov				
Riane Richard				
Rohan Ayachit				
Samijo Buczeksmith				
Sarah Davis				
Shadeh Din				
Varun Mondaiyka				

Guidelines for Choosing Stories to Share with Interfaith Audiences

Compiled by Staff of Children at the Well

- Choose [or create] a story that says something special about your culture or religion that you would like others to know. Make the story your own.
- Choose a story that you love, one that moves you and that you believe will affect others. Serious or funny, choose it because it speaks to you.
- Remember, storytelling isn't about converting others to your beliefs.
- If your story includes religious terms, references to holidays, historical events, or practices, your listeners may need a brief explanation either at the beginning or when you use the term.
- A story that imparts a piece of wisdom (sometimes called a "Wisdom Tale") or an essential truth can be a good choice.
- Acknowledge that stories from many traditions may illustrate the same truth, or impart the same wisdom.
- Always be open to the fact that others' beliefs and/or practices may be very different from yours and that great richness and insights often come because of the diversity.
- Be aware that the story you choose for an interfaith audience may be different from one you'd tell to listeners from your own tradition.
- Consider whether there is anything about the story you are choosing that might be offensive to another group of people or cause harm. Be especially careful to avoid presenting hurtful stereotypes or portraying people of a particular tradition in an unfavorable way. Tell your story to rehearsal partners and/or your group's leader with this in mind. If this seems to be a possibility, your best choice is to look for a different story to share.

Storytelling Prompts

Storytelling prompts are useful in helping students formulate a story. Often a suggestion or even just a word can give the storyteller an idea or can trigger a personal memory that he/she can build upon to create a story.

Sample Prompts for Spiritual or Religious Stories

Tell about a time when:

- you had an insight about your faith
- prayer made a difference in what happened or the way you felt
- a person of faith affected you or taught you something
- a misfortune became a blessing in disguise
- you struggled with the right thing to do and your faith helped you decide
- a scripture tale affected you or connected to something in your life
- you experienced a special tradition or a memorable holiday

Sample Prompts for Secular Stories

Tell about:

- something a relative (Mom, Dad, sister, cousin, etc.) always says or does
- an interesting experience involving an animal
- a favorite place or a secret place
- a time you cooked something that did not turn out right
- a time you were lost or scared
- an award, contest, medal, or trophy you have won
- the best or worst day you ever had in school
- a place where you used to live or a place where you would like to live

Story Choice Form

My name _____

The story I am choosing to tell is:

Title _____

Source _____

I like this story because

_____

_____

_____

This story is a good one to represent my culture or religion because

_____

_____

_____

Words or customs or traditions that I might have to explain in some way in this story are

_____

_____

_____

To me, the wisdom I find in this story is

_____

_____

_____

This story is a good one for community events because

_____

_____

_____

All Purpose C@W Event Checklist

Starting at Least Three Months Ahead

DETERMINE OVERALL BUDGET, as desired, for the venue, sound engineer and recording, supplies, rentals, additional fees, printing of fliers, programs, other advertising.

CHOOSE VENUE, keeping in mind location, parking, handicapped access, bathrooms, acoustics, noise competition, stage, lighting and ambiance, janitorial and technical help, affordability, "built-in audience." For events followed by potlucks, consider whether kitchen and dining room are available.

CHOOSE AND SCHEDULE DATE and times.

CHOOSE PERFORMERS (storytellers, musicians, dancers, etc.). Contact them to determine availability.

Determine optimal performance times and plan program accordingly, ideally aiming for two diverse sets of approximately 45 minutes each (not longer).

ENLIST A COACH TO BE STAGE MANAGER and have him or her discuss with the rest of the coaches and storytellers how things will proceed on the day of the event.

ARRANGE FOR SOUND ENGINEER/RECORDING, PHOTOGRAPHER, VIDEOGRAPHER, ETC. as desired.

ENLIST MC or decide who will speak at which points in the program.

DESIGNATE PERSON TO CREATE FLIERS (full size, color, for display and Internet use), handbills (black and white, quarter sheets for handing out), and personal invitations.

PERSONAL INVITATIONS (see above). Make a list of people to whom you would like to send invitations, and designate one person to address, sign, and send them out.

DESIGNATE PERSON OR PEOPLE TO DO PUBLICITY/PRESS OUTREACH (social media, email, newspapers, radio, TV).

HAVE AN OVERALL STRATEGY FOR PRESS CONTACT, INCLUDING TIMING:

- Write press release and distribute.
- Orchestrate distribution of fliers and handbills.
- Place any ads and/or listings (check schedule of publication well ahead).

DESIGNATE PERSON TO SELL BUSINESS ADS AND "SUNSHINE ADS" TO PLACE IN PROGRAM. Decide on size, costs. Make up a form to solicit ads, with prices AND other info. Design (if necessary) and lay out ads.

One Month Ahead

Create Program

- Collect names and brief bios of performers (ages, schools, and congregations, etc.).
- Names of stories/music/dances, including tradition, source, any explanations necessary.
- Names and info of coaches.
- Determine order of the program.
- Include in program: housekeeping info, thank-yous, donors, updates, quotations, dedications, logos. Have programs (with ads inside!) printed several days in advance.

Organize the Potluck Dinner

Enlist two people to work together as pre-event organizers who:

Call and/or email parents and other community guests

- Find out what people will bring to share at the potluck.
- Coordinate the offerings to ensure variety and consider dietary needs. Request that people bring with them a small sign listing all ingredients in the dishes they will bring.

Shop for supplies

- Paper products: plates, napkins, hot and cold cups, foil or plastic wrap, plastic ware, trash bags if needed.
- Table decorations—tablecloths if needed, flowers/balloons/other.
- For hot beverages—tea bags, hot chocolate, coffee, filters, sweeteners, honey, cream/milk, stirrers.
- Cold drinks.

Pre-event organizers need to enlist people for day of event to help

- Receive the food and keep it warm/cold.
- Set up one service table with plates, silverware, and food, and another with drinks and cups.
- Set up tables for seating, with decorations and literature (including "Just Wanted You to Know ..." forms and story prompts).
- Serve, replenish, and tidy up the food/drinks.
- Monitor the garbage situation, make sure there are adequate receptacles and trash bags, and take out trash when needed.
- Wash the bowls and pots, etc., that people have brought, and put them out on a table to be taken home.
- Clean up the kitchen and remove any additional trash.

Arrange for Help Needed the Day of the Event

Enlist people to:

- **Make a sign/signs to direct people to the event if it's in a large building, etc.**
- **Give out a cell phone number for people to call if they need directions,** are lost, etc., the day of the event. Have it be someone other than the event organizer.
- **If donations are to be collected at event,** designate one person to be in charge of the collection. The collection area should be centrally located, well indicated by signage, and announced from the stage.
- **Assign people to sit at a sign-in table at the door.** Be aware of multiple entrances, and station people at them also or arrange to keep those entrances closed, if possible. Have guests directed to the sign-in table.
- **Enlist a person to sit at literature/display table and collect mailing list info.**
- **Enlist people to sell any merchandise, such as T-shirts, CDs, etc.**
- **Enlist board members, parents, others to act as roving ambassadors,** welcoming people, sharing info on our programs. Especially to be on the lookout for people who are new to us.
- **Enlist ushers to hand out programs and help guests find seats.**
- **Enlist a person to monitor and address noise levels and other distractions "in the house" during the performance.**
- **Enlist a coach to be in charge of the Human Treasure Hunt** or other mixer activity that will happen after the performance and before the potluck.
- **Designate a leader or two for each table** at the potluck to spur conversation, lead with story prompts, and encourage people to fill out the "Just Wanted You to Know ..."

sheets (long tables need two leaders, one at each end). See "Instructions for Leaders at Potlucks" later in this appendix.

- **Designate** two people to circulate at potluck and collect the "Just Wanted You to Know …" forms.
- **Check in** with any photographer, sound engineer, videographer, etc., if you have arranged for their help.

On the Day of the Event

Plan to be there early and have on hand:

- ☐ Children at the Well banner, banner stand.
- ☐ Signs to direct guests to the event.
- ☐ If necessary, sound equipment, sound system and/or mics, lavalier mics, etc.
- ☐ Charged camera, video camera, iPhone, etc.
- ☐ Batteries, memory cards, power cords.
- ☐ Forms to collect names and email addresses for mailing list, on clipboards.
- ☐ Bunches of pens, in jars, for sign-in sheets, for Human Treasure Hunt, to put on tables for "Just Wanted You to Know …" forms.
- ☐ Tablecloths for display, merchandise, and check-in tables.
- ☐ Printed programs (with ads!).
- ☐ Human Treasure Hunt forms (mixer activity before the potluck).
- ☐ "Just Wanted You to Know …" forms (very helpful for collecting comments!) to put on tables.
- ☐ Small wrapped candies as "rewards" for handing in completed Treasure Hunt forms and "Just Wanted You to Know …" forms.
- ☐ Posters, C@W literature, info for other events, for a display on extra table.
- ☐ Items for sale: T-shirts, books, CDs, etc., with signs and something to collect cash and checks in.
- ☐ Small bills and coins to make change.
- ☐ Basket or other container for donations.
- ☐ Purse or other secure case that can be worn for stashing donations.
- ☐ Scotch tape, duct tape, Band-Aids, scissors, safety pins, etc.
- ☐ All necessary phone numbers.

Check Request Form
for Reimbursement

C@W RELATED EXPENSES

Please submit receipts along with this form for reimbursement. Thanks!

DATE	AMOUNT	WHAT WAS PURCHASED?	NOTES

Events Form

For reimbursement related to extra coaching and student participation in events
COACHING approved up to hour(s), at $/hour

Name of Coach: _____

Date: _____

Student who needs coaching: _____

Story (or stories) for which he/she needs coaching: _____

Notes: _____

Event that is being prepared for, including place and date: _____

Other event-related duties: _____

ORGANIZE STUDENT PARTICIPATION _____

PROVIDE TRANSPORTATION _____

ATTEND EVENT AND SUPERVISE STUDENT/S _____

Names of all students participating in event: _____

For coach to fill out when submitting form for reimbursement

_____

Date submitted: _____

COACHING:

About how much time did you spend coaching this student? _____

In your estimation, is the student's story ready for public telling? _____

Length of story: _____

Title of story: _____

ORGANIZED STUDENT PARTICIPATION IN EVENT: _____

PROVIDED TRANSPORT: _____

ATTENDED EVENT AND PROVIDED SUPERVISION: _____

Any Notes: _____

Instructions for Leaders at Potlucks

To the teachers and/or parents who have said yes to leading activities at the potluck, there are three specific things you can help with:

1. **Human Treasure Hunt**—After the storytelling performance, a coach will be handing out Human Treasure Hunt forms (like a Bingo card, see below for an example) and pens. It should prove to be lots of fun. It would be great if you would lead the way by engaging in this activity yourself and by encouraging all those you meet to do the same.

2. **Story prompts to be used for story-sharing at tables**—One or two leaders should be seated at each table, depending on the length of the table. Please try to position yourselves as best you can to talk with people. We're going to encourage people to sit with others they do not know—one family with another, two friends with two others, etc. We realize there is only so much we can do to achieve a mix, but please see if you can encourage this, and place yourself where you think you might be helpful.

   Find a sheet of story prompts on your table (see below for prompts) and use the prompts as a way to get people to share their stories with the table. We certainly don't want to inhibit people from having normal conversations, but we do want to encourage them to engage in meaningful story-sharing. This is just as much a part of the goal of the afternoon (and our project) as the youth telling.

3. **Just Wanted You to Know**—On the tables there will be "Just Wanted You to Know" sheets (and pens), which we would like people to add their comments to before they leave. We will be using these forms to evaluate the telling and the potluck meal—the community part of our project—in our reports. Please see that people take a moment to write their answer before they leave. It is very important to us. Thank you!

Thanks so much for being willing to help. In so many ways, as you can see, the success of the afternoon depends on those of you who are story-leading in these ways. Your efforts on our behalf are much appreciated. I know that your presence and sharing are going to make all the difference!

Human Treasure Hunt

Note: The idea for this activity came to us from storyteller Bob Kanegis, who used it in his F.E.A.S.T.! (Families Eating and Storytelling Together) program. All four versions of the Human Treasure Hunt grid on the following pages are to be handed out.

Goal: To find persons here who are a "match" for each square below. When you find them, have them print their name in the square that applies.

You may not use the same person for more than one square.

Prize: Getting to meet each other and to think about all the stories that are associated with these squares.

Find a Person Who...

Reads the Qur'an	Had a math test in school this week	Lights Shabbat candles
Knows the Hail Mary	Knows how to pronounce Mahabharata	Has a cat
Can do a cartwheel	Knows the story of Siddhartha Gautama	Is a 7th grader

Human Treasure Hunt

Goal: To find persons here who are a "match" for each square below. When you find them, have them print their name in the square that applies
You may not use the same person for more than one square.
Prize: Getting to meet each other and to think about all the stories that are associated with these squares.

Find a Person Who...

Celebrates Dwali	Has a mezuzah on their doorpost	Often says "Inshallah" (G-d willing)
Knows the seven principles	Was part of Children at the Well in 2006- the first year	Gets ashes on his or her forehead
Has prayer beads	Has been to Jerusalem	Likes latkes (potato pancakes)

Human Treasure Hunt

Goal: To find persons here who are a "match" for each square below. When you find them, have them print their name in the square that applies

You may not use the same person for more than one square

Prize: Getting to meet each other and to think about all the stories that are associated with these squares.

Find a Person Who...

Made a pilgrimage to Mecca	Can recite the Ten Commandments	Has a statue of Buddha
Belongs to an inter–faith family	Knows what a flower communion is	Likes fava beans
Worships on Sunday	Plays the piano	Is a vegetarian

Human Treasure Hunt

Goal: To find persons here who are a "match" for each square below. When you find them, have them print their name in the square that applies

You may not use the same person for more than one square.

Prize: Getting to meet each other and to think about all the stories that are associated with these squares.

Find a Person Who...

Knows about the Noble Eight-Fold Path	Fasts during Yom Kippur	Likes hot fudge sundaes
Fasts during Lent	Hasn't warmed up yet from our cold, cold winter	Fasts during Ramadan
Has gone to an Inter-faith Story Circle	Is familiar with the symbol of the flaming chalice	Is an 8th grader

Prompts for Story-Sharing at Potlucks

This list of prompts can be printed (or pasted) on both sides of folded tent cards to stand on the tables.

- Tell the story of what brought you here today.
- Which story told by the students today held the most meaning for you?
- Did any of the students' stories remind you of another story that you know?
- Is there a story behind your name?
- Are there any stories that you thought of, or heard, when you were filling in the Human Treasure Hunt squares?
- Do you have a story about one of your family's holiday customs?
- Do you have a funny or really unusual story?
- What is your favorite story from your family or cultural traditions?

"Just Wanted You To Know ..." Form

We've found that a good size for this is half a sheet of 8 ½ inch by 11 inch paper. Print two to a page, and cut.

"Here in Our Circle" Song

by Paul Strausman
© 2007

Born at the dawn of time
Passed down from heart to mind
Here where our stories all entwine
The past and the future meet
In all of our hopes and dreams
The circle of wisdom is now complete

CHORUS:
Hand to hand
(Here in our circle)
Heart to mind
(Here in our circle)
The stories are yours and mine
Here in our circle
Spinning through time

Time builds the bridge we cross
That carries us back to the source
Voices from the past are never lost
The promise is ours to keep
The well is so rich and deep
As we sow so shall we reap

Completer Statements

These can be used occasionally at the end of a session to encourage students to reflect on and describe their reactions to the activities they have engaged in.

DATE: _____

Please choose three statements to complete:
IN RELATION TO TODAY'S SESSION:

I WAS SURPRISED…

I NOTICED…

I FELT…

I REALIZED…

THE SESSION MADE ME THINK ABOUT…

ONE QUESTION I HAVE IS…

ONE SUGGESTION I WOULD MAKE IS…

I JUST WANTED YOU TO KNOW…

C@W Project Survey

This was used some years as a pre- and post-program survey in an attempt to collect effectiveness data for the purposes of program development and grant writing.

Name: _____

Rate yourself as you see yourself *today* on a scale of 1 to 5 (5 being the highest).

Circle your answers, and put any comments below the question or on the back of the page.

1. I know about religious traditions other than my own.	1	2	3	4	5
2. I have had personal experiences with people of other faith traditions.	1	2	3	4	5
3. I am comfortable sharing stories with people of other traditions.	1	2	3	4	5
4. I understand that storytelling is a way to teach others.	1	2	3	4	5
5. I already know and use stories from other traditions.	1	2	3	4	5
6. I know how to help people get something from a story.	1	2	3	4	5
7. I encourage others to share stories.	1	2	3	4	5
8. I am familiar with where to find stories.	1	2	3	4	5
9. I see myself as a storyteller.	1	2	3	4	5
10. I understand what makes a skillful storyteller.	1	2	3	4	5

Use the back if you have anything else you'd like to tell us! Thanks.

Sample Travel Permission Form

I understand that my child will travel to and from Northeastern University, Boston, in a motor vehicle operated by a Children at the Well staff person or volunteer for the purpose of participating in the TIDE Conference of Interfaith Action from Friday May 27th to Sunday May 29th, 2011. This person is a licensed and insured driver, and I clearly understand the risks associated with my child's travel and assume all risks thereof.

Printed Name of Parent/Legal Guardian: _____

Signature of Parent/Legal Guardian: _____

Date: _____

I hereby authorize Paula Weiss and/or Kay Hebert to stand in loco parentis and authorize any necessary medical care or treatment should I be unavailable to render such consent for my minor child/student myself. I either have appropriate insurance or, in its absence, I agree to pay all costs of medical services as may be incurred on my/our behalf.

Signature of Parent/Legal Guardian: _____

Date: _____

Contact Information

Parent/Legal Guardian Name: _____

Home Telephone Number: _____

Cell Phone Number: _____

Work Telephone Number: _____

Alternate Emergency Contact Name: _____

Relationship to Participant: _____

Home Telephone Number: _____

Cell Phone Number: _____

Work Telephone Number: _____

Sample Travel Permission Form, Medical Information

If there are special instructions please include a separate note or call Director

- Allergies:

  _____

  _____

- Is student taking any medications or supplements?

  _____

- Does student have a medically prescribed diet? _____ If so, list needs below:

  _____

  _____

- Any physical limitations?

  _____

- Date of last tetanus booster: _____
- Note any special medical conditions:

  _____

  _____

  _____

Insurance Carrier _____   Policy Carrier _____

Policy Number: _____

Name of Student's Physician: _____

Phone Number for Student's Physician: _____

Sample Performance Program

Welcome to our garden

...the tenth C@W performance!

Sunday, April 26 th, 2015

2 PM

First Unitarian Universalist Society of Albany

405 Washington Ave.

Stories matter. Many stories matter. Stories have been used to dispossess and to malign, but stories can also be used to empower and to humanize. Stories can break the dignity of a people, but stories can also repair that broken dignity...
When we reject the single story, when we realize that there is never a single story about any place, we regain a kind of paradise.

-Chimamanda Ngozi Adichie, novelist

What a garden the world would be if storytelling by children from different faith groups became a way of understanding each other.

-Jyoti Swaminathan, PhD

interfaithstory.org/tricity

Some of what C@W has been up to lately:

In 2015:

- We moved our coaching meetings to Albany
- We became members of the Brave New Voices Network of Youth Speaks and were invited to attend Convening in San Francisco
- We were joined by two new assistant coaches, Allison and Danielle
- Ben Russell, an original C@W student, became a full coach
- We are assembling a C@W Guide to enable others to start similar programs nationwide!

Children at the Well is supported, in part, by the Seymour Fox Memorial Foundation, the Suozzo Family, and Stewarts Shops

With many, many thanks to:
Children at the Well parents;as always, the best!
Our wonderful coaching staff: Nancy, Micki, Ben, Danielle and Allison
Our past storycoaches: Mary Murphy, Marni Gillard, Claire Nolan
Our co-founder and past director: Gert Johnson
Kate Dudding, webmaster
The board of our parent organization, theInterfaith Story Circle: Audrey Seidman, Linda Russell, Mussarat Chaudhry, Claire Nolan, Sharifa Din, Paula Weiss
Our inspiring visitors this year:Eliud Nieves, Beth Novik, Jacqui Williams, Marni Gillard...Jyoti Swaminathan was on our schedule but the snows of 2015 made a raincheck necessary. Next year, Jyoti!
Our indomitable C@W storytellers from 2006 to today!
Additional important "Thank Yous" are onthe inside cover of this program
→ Please sign up to walk with us in the **Freihofer's Community Walk 2015**!
Contact Linda-lindamrussell@gmail.com-or Sumit-mondy_01@yahoo.com

On Facebook, please "like" the Children at the Well Fan Page

Welcome: Paula Weiss, director

Master of Ceremonies: Ben Russell, storycoach

Candle lighting

Stories:

Kate Dudding, storyteller and story producer, C@W webmaster and friend; *One Path to World Peace*, an original story with which Kate won the 2010 National Storytelling Network story slam!

Samijo Buczeksmith, 10th grade, Bethlehem High School, Unitarian; *Strega Nona and the Pasta Pot*

Atharv Agashe, 11, 6th grade, Latham Ridge Elementary School; *The Three Doubts*, a folk tale from India

Varun Mondaiyka, 7th grade, Shaker Junior High School; *Maha Danav*, and Indian folk tale

Intermission: Micki Groper, storycoach

~~~ A Ten Minute Stretch Break ~~~

Welcome Back: Ben Russell

Indian Classical Dance by students of Narthanalaya School of Arts, led by Sujatha Sundar

Prayer to some of the Hindu Deities in the form of hymns called Bhajans

Ganesha Anjali; This first dance is a prayer to the Elephant Headed Lord Ganesha, the remover of all obstacles
Dancers: Aditri Gupta, Bhargavi Ramamurthy, Shruthi Lalukota, Shruti Kamat, Sreehitha Manga, and Veda Nandikam.

Slokams; a depiction of different aspects of the deities. They are prayed to for protection from unknown obstacles, wisdom and knowledge, auspiciousness and peace.

Dancers: Lasya Penumalli, Pranali Rodda, Shreya Sharath, Shreeya Gillela, Shriya Arunkumar, Shriya Penumalli, Shruthika Manga

Kalaimagal Kautuvam; a prayer to Goddess Saraswathi, who is the goddess of knowledge and arts. Through this dance she is thanked for teaching the various aspects of dance: Expressions, Hand Gestures (Mudras) and Karnas (Postures)

Dancers: Kavipriya Kovai Palanivel, Riane Nikita Richard, Rishita Nagothi, Ruchika Kilaparty, Shrutthi Kannaathaal

Stories:

Shadeh Din, Muslim, 18, 12th grade, South Colonie High School; *Nuristan,* a modern day story of Shadeh's family's village in Afghanistan,

Rohan Ayachit, 16, 10th grade, Shenendehowa High School; *The Wish Ring,* a retelling of a story by a German physician, Richard Volksmann-Leander

Sarah Davis, 18, 12th grade, Columbia High School. Sarah grew up in a Catholic and Jewish household; *The Little Match Girl,* from the story by Hans Christian Andersen

Kalyan Ramkumar, 16, 11th grade, Bethlehem High School; *Subban the Astrologer,* an Indian folk tale

Presentation to seniors: Nancy Marie Payne, storycoach
Curtain Call: all 2015 participants
Alumni bow: All C@W Alumni will be called up to take a bow
[*Photo Ops!!*]

Our storycoaches; Nancy Marie Payne,

Micki Groper, and Ben Russell

Assistant coaches; Danielle Charlestin and Allison Lerman-Gluck

Recommended Resources

Books

Baum, Noa. 2016. *A Land Twice Promised: An Israeli Woman's Quest for Peace*. Familius.

Chace, Karen. 2014. *Story by Story*. Marion, MI: Parkhurst Brothers Inc.

Cordi, Kevin D. 2014. *Playing with Stories: Story Crafting For Writers, Teachers, and Other Imaginative Thinkers*. Marion, MI: Parkhurst Brothers Inc.

Kirchner, Suzie Linton. 1981. *Signs for All Seasons: More Sign Language Games*. Northridge, CA: Joyce Media, Inc.

Lipman, Doug. 1995. *The Storytelling Coach: How to Listen, Praise, And Bring out People's Best*. Little Rock: August House.

Lipman, Doug. 1999. *Improving Your Storytelling: Beyond the Basics for All Who Tell Stories in Work or Play*. Little Rock: August House.

Gillard, Marni. 1996. *Storyteller, Storyteacher: Discovering the Power of Storytelling for Teaching and Living*. York, Maine: Stenhouse Publishers.

Sima, Judy, and Kevin D. Cordi. 2003. *Raising Voices: Creating youth storytelling groups and troupes*. Westport, Conn.: Libraries Unlimited.

Books Containing Very Short Stories

Feldman, Christina and Jack Kornfield. 1996. *Soul Food: Stories to Nourish the Spirit and Heart*. New York: HarperCollins.

Henderson, Florence and Shari Lewis. 1986. *One-Minute Bible Stories: New Testament*. Garden City, NY: Doubleday Books for Young Readers.

Lewis, Shari. 1985. *One-Minute Favorite Fairy Tales*. Garden City, NY: Doubleday Books for Young Readers.

Lewis, Shari. 1986. *One-Minute Bible Stories: Old Testament*. Garden City, NY: Doubleday Books for Young Readers.

Lewis, Shari. 1987. *One-Minute Christmas Stories*. Garden City, NY: Doubleday Books for Young Readers.

Lewis, Shari. 1987. *One-minute Greek Myths*. Garden City, NY: Doubleday Books for Young Readers.

Lewis, Shari. 1989. *One-minute Jewish Stories*. Garden City, NY: Doubleday Books for Young Readers.

MacDonald, Margaret Read. 1992. *Peace Tales: World Folktales to Talk About*. New Haven, CT.: Linnet Books.

MacDonald, Margaret Read. 2004. *Three Minute Tales: Stories from Around the World*. Little Rock, Ark.: August House.

MacDonald, Margaret Read. 2007. *Five Minute Tales: Stories from Around the World*. Little Rock, Ark.: August House.

Pearmain, Elisa Davy. 2007. *Doorways to the Soul: 52 Wisdom Tales from Around the World*. Eugene, Ore.: Resource Publications.

Shannon, George and Sis, Peter. 2000. *Stories to Solve: Fifteen Folktales from Around the World*. Greenwillow.

Shannon, George and Sis, Peter. 2001. *More Stories to Solve: Fifteen Folktales from Around the World*. Greenwillow.

Simms, Laura. 2013. *Stories to Nourish the Hearts of Our Children*. New York: Laura Simms Storyteller.

Websites

These websites offer a wealth of information about using storytelling to address issues of diversity and social justice, effect personal and social change, and develop leadership skills in young people.

Susan O'Halloran, racebridgesstudio.com and susanohalloran.com/resources

Lani Peterson, lanipeterson.com

Interfaith Youth Core, www.ifyc.org/faculty/library

The Interfaith Observer is a free monthly digital journal created to explore interreligious relations and the interfaith movement, www.theinterfaithobserver.org

Storytellers

Some storytellers whose work involves interfaith understanding:

Kate Dudding, www.katedudding.com

Pam Faro, storycrossings.com

Cindy Rivka Marshall, www.cindymarshall.com

Susan Stone, Keeping Faith: Sisters of Story, susanstone-storyteller.com

Storytelling for Social Justice and Community Awareness

Sheila Arnold, www.mssheila.org

Nicolette Nordin Heavey, Stories in the Streets, www.nicolettestories.com/stories-in-a-st/

Jennifer Rudick Zunikoff, The Golden Door Storytelling, www.facebook.com/TheGolden DoorStorytelling

Jacqui C. Williams, Filling in the Gaps in American History (FIGAH), Inc., www.facebook.com/pg/FIGAH.US

Video

Lyden, John. *Stepping Toward the Lion; finding my story*. 2013. www.lydenproductions.com This film by C@W alum John Lyden chronicles the journey of Alaudeen, a young African-American Muslim, as he ventures through the C@W program and gains a new perspective on life after dealing with years of prejudice and bullying. Storytelling enables Alaudeen to better understand and overcome the one major obstacle that stands between him and his future: his fear. (31 minutes)

To view the film, please see www.childrenatthewell.org/our-stories-connect for instructions.

Supportive Organizations

This is a list of many of the organizations with which C@W has connected and from which we have received support. Some are national or regional organizations, though most are in or near our area, the Capital Region of New York. Consider the opportunities and resources that may be available for your program in your own community.

Storytelling and Other Spoken Word Organizations

National Storytelling Network (NSN), www.storynet.org/
Northeast Storytelling, www.nestorytelling.org
Interfaith Story Circle (Albany, Schenectady, and Troy, New York), www.withourvoice.org/ifsc/
Story Circle of the Capital District, www.storycircleatproctors.org/sc/Articles.shtml
Brave New Voices Network of Youth Speaks, youthspeaks.org/bravenewvoices/

Funding Organizations

Arts Center of the Capital Region, New York, www.artscenteronline.org
Seymour Fox Memorial Foundation, Troy, New York, www.seymourfoxfoundation.org
Chobani Foundation, www.chobani.com/foundation
Suozzo Family Foundation
Stewart's Shops, www.stewartsshops.com/contributions/
Freihofer's Charitable Partners Program (formerly "Community Walk"), Albany, New York, www.freihofersrun.com/charitable-partners/

C@W has also received donations from many individuals, from a church grant and church collections, and from clergy discretionary funds.

Development and Support

Community Foundation for the Greater Capital Region, Albany, New York, www.cfgcr.org/
The New York Council of Nonprofits, Inc., Albany, New York, nycon.org

Interfaith Organizations

Interfaith Community of Schenectady, schenectadyinterfaith.weebly.com

Interfaith Center of the State University of New York at Albany, www.albanyinterfaith-center.org

Sidney and Beatrice Alpert Lectureship series, College of St. Rose, Albany, New York, www.strose.edu/student-life/spiritual-life/sidney-beatrice-albert-lecture/

Interfaith Story Circle, Duchess County Interfaith Council—Poughkeepsie, New York, www.dutchesscountyinterfaith.org

Interfaith Youth Core, Chicago, Illinois, www.ifyc.org

Hickey Center for Interfaith Studies and Dialogue, Nazareth College, Rochester, New York, www2.naz.edu/interfaith/

Global Citizenship Conference www2.naz.edu/interfaith/programs/workshops-training/global-citizenship-conference/

Youth Leaders Engaging Across Differences (Youth LEAD), Sharon Massachusetts, http://www.youthleadonline.org/

Youth LEAD's TIDE Conference, Boston, Massachusetts, www.youthleadonline.org/tide-conference

Festivals

Old Songs Festival, Altamont, New York, festival.oldsongs.org

Great Hudson River Revival's Clearwater Music and Environmental Festival, Croton-on-Hudson, New York, www.clearwaterfestival.org. Barry Marshall and Jeri Burns (The Storycrafters) manage the festival's Story Grove.

Connecticut Storytelling Festival, New London, Connecticut, www.connstorycenter.org/festival.htm

Timpanogos Storytelling Festival, Lehigh, Utah, timpfest.org

Although not currently running, the Mohegan Colony Storytelling and Music Festival, Crompond, NY, produced by Judith Heineman, introduced us to a number of great contacts and friends.

Rehearsal and Performance Venues

A number of local schools, theaters, colleges, public libraries, places of worship, and cultural organizations have donated space and offered logistical support for coaching sessions, workshops, and performances—most notably, Christ Our Light Catholic Church in Loudonville, New York.

About Cohoes Falls Media

Cohoes Falls Media is the publishing imprint of WithOurVoice, Inc. Its name was inspired by the following legend:

The Peacemaker's Journey

Some say it was a thousand years ago. Some say that it was two thousand years when there was a dark period in the history of The People. The Mohawk, Oneida, Onondaga, Cayuga and Seneca Nations were at war with one another. It was a terrible time of cruelty, bloodshed and mourning. But then a Huron man, referred to as the Peacemaker, canoed from the western shore of Lake Ontario. He brought with him a message of peace and unity.

The first individual to accept his message of peace was a Seneca woman named Jigonsaseh. Because it was a woman who was the first individual to accept his message of peace, the Peacemaker gave women an important role in the new confederacy that was to be formed. Jigonsaseh became known as "The Mother of Nations."

The first nation to accept the Peacemaker's message was the Kanienkehaka or the Mohawk Nation. The Peacemaker traveled east and camped near Cohoes Falls. He made a campfire so that the Mohawks in the nearby village would see the smoke and know that he was there and that he wished to confer with them. Mohawk runners came to his campsite to ask who he was and to find out what he wanted. The Peacemaker said that he was the one they were waiting for. He was the one who was carrying a message of Peace.

The Mohawks were uncertain as to whether they should trust this stranger or not and so they said that he would have to pass a test to prove that he had the power to carry such an important message. They said that he would have to climb a tree that was growing next to Cohoes Falls. The Mohawks would then cut the tree down and if he survived the fall, they would know that he had great power and they would listen to his words. The Peacemaker agreed to the test. He climbed the tree. The tree was cut down. The Peacemaker fell into the water and disappeared over the falls. The Mohawks waited and waited, but there was no sign of the visitor emerging from the water. The Mohawks were disappointed and went back to their village.

The next morning, a thin wisp of white smoke was seen in the distance. Upon investigation, it was discovered that the Peacemaker had made this campfire and that he was alive and well. He was waiting to be invited to enter the village. It was in that village that he met Ayonwatha, the one who would travel with him to convince the five nations to stop fighting and to unify.

It took many years, but eventually, the Mohawk, Oneida, Onondaga, Cayuga and Seneca Nations unified and formed a peace league. The English referred to it as "The Five Nations." Later, they called it "The Six Nations" because the Tuscarora people came north from the Carolinas in the early 1700s to join. The French called the league "The Iroquois Confederacy." The real name is the "Haudenosaunee" meaning "The People of the Longhouse" which refers to the traditional long, bark-covered houses in which the Haudenosaunee lived.

Reprinted with the permission of the Iroquois Indian Museum